C. PETER WAGNER

WHAT THE BIBLE SAYS ABOUT
SPIRITUAL
WARFARE

Regal

From Gospel Light
Ventura, California, U.S.A.

Published by Regal Books
Gospel Light
Ventura, California, U.S.A.
Printed in the U.S.A.

Regal Books is a ministry of Gospel Light, an evangelical Christian publisher dedicated to serving the local church. We believe God's vision for Gospel Light is to provide church leaders with biblical, user-friendly materials that will help them evangelize, disciple and minister to children, youth and families.

It is our prayer that this Regal book will help you discover biblical truth for your own life and help you meet the needs of others. May God richly bless you.

For a free catalog of resources from Regal Books/Gospel Light, please call your Christian supplier or contact us at 1-800-4-GOSPEL *or* www.regalbooks.com.

Cover and Interior Design by Robert Williams
Edited by Julie Carobini and Rose Decaen

Library of Congress Cataloging-in-Publication Data
Wagner, C. Peter
    The spiritual warfare answer book/C. Peter Wagner.
      p. cm.
    Includes bibliographical references.
    ISBN 0-8307-2906-2 (trade)
1. Spiritual warfare—Miscellanea. 2. Demonology—Miscellanea. I. Title.

BT975 .W26 2002
235'.4—dc21
                                        2001051093

1 2 3 4 5 6 7 8 9 10 11 12 13 14 15 / 09 08 07 06 05 04 03 02 01

Rights for publishing this book in other languages are contracted by Gospel Light Worldwide, the international nonprofit ministry of Gospel Light. Gospel Light Worldwide also provides publishing and technical assistance to international publishers dedicated to producing Sunday School and Vacation Bible School curricula and books in the languages of the world. For additional information, visit www.gospellightworldwide.org; write to Gospel Light Worldwide, P.O. Box 3875, Ventura, CA 93006; or send an e-mail to info@gospellightworldwide.org.

Contents

BEFORE WE GET TO THE QUESTIONS

The decade of the 1990s was an extraordinary period of time in the sweep of Christian history. With the possible exceptions of the decade in which Constantine became the emperor of Rome and the decade in which Luther nailed his 95 Theses to the door of the Wittenberg cathedral, it could be argued that no other decade since Jesus' resurrection has seen greater changes in the Church.

One of those radical changes, among many others, was the introduction of principles and techniques of strategic-level spiritual warfare into a broad segment of the Body of Christ. Before the 1990s the term "strategic-level spiritual warfare" had not even been coined. The same is true of cognitive terms such as "spiritual mapping," "identificational repentance," "prophetic intercession" and "territorial commitment"—all of which are now in common usage here in the twenty-first century.

Lausanne II in Manila

The seed thoughts for using aggressive spiritual warfare as a component of strategies of world evangelization were planted in the historic Lausanne II Congress held in Manila, Philippines, in 1989. Five of the workshops in Manila, done by recognized world leaders, turned out to be on the subject of "territorial spirits," a topic which most of the 4,500 invited delegates from all nations had not previously thought much about. I happened to do one of those workshops, and it seemed to fall to my lot to follow up on these new ideas after the congress. To be honest, I sensed during that meeting that the Lord had spoken directly to me with the assignment of taking future leadership in the field of what was to become known as strategic-level spiritual warfare.

The following year, 1990, saw the first meeting of about 25 of us who became charter members of the United States Spiritual Warfare Network. For three years we met privately twice a year just to hear each other and to pray for God's guidance as to how we should inform the Body of Christ about what God had been showing us. In 1991 Luis Bush invited me to serve as the coordinator of the AD2000 United Prayer Track, and he agreed that I should bring the Spiritual Warfare Network (SWN) into the AD2000 Movement. The SWN decided to make public its findings on an international scale during the Gideon's Army meeting in Seoul, Korea, in 1993. Subsequently, it grew considerably throughout the decade. The high point was the Celebration Ephesus meeting in 1999 in which 5,000 of us from 62 nations gathered in the amphitheater in ancient Ephesus, Turkey, for four hours of prayer and praise to Jesus.

The Literature
During the decade a small library of books on strategic-level spiritual warfare was published and widely distributed. A sampling of some of the outstanding works includes the following:

- *Taking Our Cities for God* by John Dawson—the initial wake-up call for the whole Church.
- *Territorial Spirits*, edited by C. Peter Wagner (also published as *Engaging the Enemy*)—a compilation of writings of several leaders who had been saying things related to territorial spirits before 1990.
- *Possessing the Gates of the Enemy* by Cindy Jacobs—a manual for militant intercession.
- *Warfare Prayer* by C. Peter Wagner—a guide to the basic concepts and methodologies of strategic-level spiritual warfare.
- *The Jericho Hour* by Dick Eastman—case studies of how strategic-level spiritual warfare has advanced the cause of evangelism.
- *The House of the Lord* by Francis Frangipane—how and why the whole Body of Christ should take spiritual warfare for our cities seriously.

- *Commitment to Conquer* by Bob Beckett—the textbook on territorial commitment and why it is effective for city transformation.
- *Confronting the Powers* by C. Peter Wagner—an answer to common arguments raised against strategic-level spiritual warfare.
- *Healing America's Wounds* by John Dawson—the principal guide to the why and how of identificational repentance.
- *God At War: The Bible and Spiritual Conflict* by Gregory A. Boyd—written by a Bethel College theologian, a scholarly textbook on spiritual warfare with a new view of how the providence of God comes into play.
- *Informed Intercession* by George Otis, Jr.—the most mature and thorough textbook on spiritual mapping.

As you can see, interest in spiritual warfare has been skyrocketing. Large segments of the Church, across many denominational lines, practice spiritual warfare in different ways. Growing numbers of missionaries are now realizing that they stand to see more fruit from their labors if they precede their efforts for the ground war in the visible world with an effective air war in the invisible world. Seminaries and Bible schools are adding courses on spiritual warfare to their curricula.

Underlying Issues
Still, as might be expected, not all agree with this trend.

Some Church leaders question whether demonic personalities even exist at all. They are more comfortable with the notion that impersonal forces emerging from human decisions and social dynamics cause the evil around all of us. Belief in demons seems to them to be a residue of medieval superstition, not belonging to a realistic modern worldview.

If I am not mistaken, however, the trend today seems to be away from skepticism concerning demons. Many more pastors and other leaders representing various theological streams are now affirming that personal beings, called angels and demons, actually do exist in the invisible world. Yet certain ones of those who do believe in demons are not convinced that demons have been organized into some hierarchy of darkness. For some who do agree that there may be a hierarchy of sorts out there, it still does not necessarily follow that Satan has assigned principalities to attach themselves to geographical territories, physical objects such as mountains or trees, or human social networks.

Even if we grant that demonic principalities might be assigned to territories, others argue that there is relatively little biblical evidence that believers have been given authority to confront them in a proactive, offensive mode. We may defend ourselves, they say, if demons choose to attack us; but we should not do battle with demonic forces which have not attached themselves to human beings. According to this school of thought, such activity exceeds the limits of our divine authority and makes us susceptible to becoming needless casualties of war.

Innovations Tend to Generate Heat

We should not be surprised that these underlying issues of spiritual warfare continue to be vigorously discussed in books, articles, classrooms, conferences, consultations and pulpits. As I have said, strategic-level spiritual warfare is a fairly recent concept. It is an "innovation." Social science has developed a theory explaining the diffusion of innovation which helps us to regard as fairly normal some of the heated reactions to spiritual warfare that we have been seeing.

When important new ideas, or innovations, are introduced into social networks (in this case the Body of Christ), a predictable process is set in motion. This process ordinarily produces four types of responses after the innovators themselves introduce the new idea or product.

Those who typify the first type of reaction are known as early adopters. When the innovation first becomes known, early adopters say, "This is exactly what I have been waiting for!" It meets a need, they accept it, and they begin to tell their friends. This happened, for example, with the introduction of the horseless carriage, Sunday School, hybrid corn, Social Security, sliced bread, pantyhose and thousands of other innovations that have now become commonplace in our daily lives.

But while the early adopters are trying to spread the word, different degrees of controversy usually erupt. People are not used to the new thing. It tends to pull them out of their comfort zones. Change becomes a threat to them. This happened, for example, with the innovation of the automobile. The first ones who dared to drive a Model T Ford through the streets of their towns often found their behavior quite unpopular with the majority—for a time, that is. The most intense controversy over an innovation is generated in the early adoption stage. This is all to the good because it encourages valuable corrections and much fine-tuning early on in the process.

There is no set time for the duration of this early adoption stage. It will vary from innovation to innovation. But if the innovation is worthwhile, it eventually begins to appeal to the middle adopters. Here is where the most rapid growth occurs. The controversy has cooled off, glitches have been worked out, and a favorable attitude emerges.

When the growth period slows and begins to plateau, a number of late adopters may eventually accept the innovation. But not all will. The final group identified in the theory of diffusion of innovation is composed of so-called laggards, who, no matter what, have decided to reject the innovation. A well-known case in point are the Amish, who have no intention of adopting the horseless carriage as an approved mode of transportation.

Controversy Generates Understanding

While the predictable controversy that surfaces during the process of considering an innovation can, and often does, leave behind a residue of bruised emotions and weakened relationships, the total outcome is, more often than not, positive.

Although some time has passed since then, I clearly recall the heated controversy that erupted among Evangelicals when John Wimber and I began teaching a course entitled "Signs, Wonders and Church Growth" at Fuller Seminary in the early 1980s. Some did not think it was appropriate to teach seminary students how to heal the sick and cast out demons, while others agreed with us that it was. We quickly moved from the early adoption stage to the middle adoption stage and we began to set seminary records for attendance in elective courses. This upset the theology faculty so much that they, for the first time in the history of the seminary, denied credit to theology students who took my course. I mention this as an example, because it is now hard to believe that healing the sick could cause so much fuss. We have passed the middle adoption stage, and today it is rare to find those in evangelical churches who oppose overt prayers for divine healing and ministries of the miraculous.

During the process of heated controversy in the middle adoption stage, those of us who were the innovators were forced to think through our positions and the way we verbalized them much more rigorously than we would have if there had been no opposition. This helped us move more rapidly than otherwise into the final stage of middle adoption in which we find ourselves now.

Strategic-Level Spiritual Warfare

It was 10 years after beginning the signs-and-wonders process that some of us began suggesting that strategic-level spiritual warfare might help advance the cause of world evangelization. Strategic-level spiritual warfare advocates aggressive spiritual confrontation with cosmic powers of darkness. My sense is that, as this book goes to press, we are in the final stage of middle adoption and ready to transition to late adoption. This means, among other things, that the controversy is cooling off. It has been a very productive season for the Body of Christ. As one of the innovators, I am grateful to the skeptics and cynics who forced me to reexamine my presuppositions and to refine my conclusions.

This book comes at a time when there is little new to add to the decade-long dialogue. Just about all of the possible questions have been raised and answered. Most Christian leaders who have tuned in to this process have now decided whether they like the answers or not. In this late adoption stage, few who do not like the answers and who therefore have rejected strategic-level spiritual warfare will change and jump aboard. I do not suppose that many of them will buy and read this book.

Why Am I Writing This Book?

The generation that ushered in the twenty-first century is the first generation in human history to have the realistic potential of completing the Great Commission. Many factors have contributed to our ability to make such an awesome statement, not the least of which is the vast army of God that was raised up during the 1990s. More people than ever before are prepared to go all the way with God. They understand that taking people "from darkness to light, and from the power of Satan to God," as the Lord commanded Saul on the Damascus Road (Acts 26:18), will be a battle. Satan does not give up anyone whom he has under his power without a fight. Evangelizing the world implies serious spiritual warfare.

No responsible general would send ground troops into battle without first controlling the air. Likewise, we must not send evangelists, missionaries, church planters and pastors into the evangelistic harvest fields without first pushing back the satanic forces of darkness that will do everything possible to keep people from hearing and believing the gospel. This is the assignment of the intercessors, and their number has multiplied incredibly over the past few years.

If we are going to get the job done, we need to be on the same page in our understanding of what we are doing and why. This book is an operations manual for the army of God that has already agreed to participate in the battle against invisible forces of evil. Not only will it help us understand more precisely what God has assigned us to do, but it will also help the ground troops comprehend what a vital role strategic-level spiritual warfare can play in assuring them of a bountiful harvest of souls.

I have distilled and collated the major issues concerning the validity of strategic-level spiritual warfare into 21 questions. These questions and their answers will assure us that we are hearing what the Spirit is saying to the churches and will give us a basis for moving to new and more effective levels of fulfilling our role toward the completion of the Great Commission.

How does strategic-level spiritual warfare differ from other types of spiritual warfare?

In the introduction to this book, I mentioned the formation of the United States Spiritual Warfare Network (USSWN) in 1990. (Incidentally, the USSWN expanded in 1993 to become the International Spiritual Warfare Network, and in 2000 the name was changed to Strategic Prayer Network [SPN].) When we began meeting, one of the first things that we agreed upon was the need for a simple taxonomy of spiritual warfare. As we discussed this with each other, it became evident that we were talking about spiritual warfare on three different levels, one of which was strategic-level spiritual warfare.

Types of Spiritual Warfare

Here is the accepted terminology:

- *Ground-level spiritual warfare.* This is commonly known as deliverance, or casting out demons. When Jesus sent out His followers, He almost always told them to heal the sick and cast out demons. Deliverance ministry is at a relatively low level in churches in the United States these days. In contrast, churches in some other parts of the world have intense deliverance ministries. One church in Colombia, for example, requires all new members to go on a weekend retreat where deliverance is available for all who need it. In Nepal, many churches would testify that no less than 100 percent of their church membership has been delivered from demons. A number of Christian leaders are determined to lift deliverance to a new level in our American churches. I recommend Doris Wagner's *How to Cast Out Demons: A Guide to the Basics* as an excellent entry-level introduction to ground-level spiritual warfare.[1]

- *Occult-level spiritual warfare.* Whereas ground-level spiritual warfare deals with demons who frequently are acting on their own, occult-level spiritual warfare faces a more organized kind of demonic influence. Those called to occult-level spiritual warfare confront demonic forces at work in witchcraft, Satanism, New Age, shamanism,

Freemasonry, spiritism, Eastern religions, voodoo, Santería and any number of other such manifestations of the power of the devil and his dark angels. Of all three levels of spiritual warfare, occult-level spiritual warfare may be our weakest area to date. Cindy Jacobs's new book, *Deliver Us from Evil*, should help move us strongly in the right direction.[2]

- *Strategic-level spiritual warfare.* This deals with the higher-ranking powers of darkness assigned to geographical territories or to significant human social networks. The term "territorial spirits" is frequently used to describe these dark angels. The 21 questions in this book are addressed to spiritual warfare on this level.

While conceptualizing these three levels of spiritual warfare is an immense help when God calls us to focus our ministry on one or the other, at the same time we need to realize that there are not three separate divisions in the invisible world of darkness. In other words, what happens on any one of the three levels has ripple effects on the other two. A good example of this is the record of the apostle Paul's evangelistic ministry in Ephesus.

Spiritual Warfare in Ephesus

Actually, Paul enjoyed more evangelistic success in Ephesus than anywhere else he went to preach the gospel. Why? I'm sure that one of the major reasons was that in Ephesus, spiritual warfare was taking place on all three levels, according to Acts 19. On the ground level, demons were being cast out by using handkerchiefs which received a divine anointing simply by touching Paul's body (see Acts 19:12). On the occult level, Ephesus happened to be the central headquarters in the Roman Empire for magic and magicians. So many magicians got saved and decided to burn their books and occult paraphernalia publicly that the items in the fire were valued at 50,000 pieces of silver (see Acts 19:19). In the research for my commentary on Acts, *Acts of the Holy Spirit*, I calculated a current equivalent of $4 million going up in flames![3]

The territorial spirit assigned by Satan to hold the people in Ephesus in spiritual darkness was Diana of the Ephesians. Some say that she might have been the most worshiped deity in the Roman Empire at the time. Her temple has gone down in history as one of the seven wonders of the ancient world. During Paul's time there, her power was shattered to the extent that, in two years, everyone not only in the city of Ephesus but also in the whole province of Asia Minor had heard the gospel (see Acts 19:10). This is notable because Paul apparently did not engage Diana in any direct strategic-level spiritual confrontation (see Acts 19:37).

How, then, was the evil power of Diana of the Ephesians broken?

It was caused by what I referred to earlier as the ripple effect of spiritual warfare done at any level. We know for a fact that demons were cast out and that magicians came to

Christ and burned their books in Ephesus. When it comes right down to it, Diana was the demonic supervisor in charge of seeing that those very demons and magicians served the purposes of Satan. When the gospel began bringing Ephesian people from the power of Satan to God, Diana began losing the spiritual authority that she had enjoyed for hundreds of years. Ground-level spiritual warfare and occult-level spiritual warfare had a devastating effect on the strategic level. The net result was a bountiful evangelistic harvest. "The word of the Lord grew mightily and prevailed" (Acts 19:20).

Before moving on to the next question, we might note that history (not the Bible) records that the apostle John later went to live in Ephesus and that while there, he did confront the weakened Diana of the Ephesians directly. In his scholarly work *The Christianization of the Roman Empire A.D. 100-400*, Yale University historian Ramsay MacMullen records that John went into Diana's temple. He writes, "In the very temple of [Diana herself], [John] prayed, 'O God . . . at whose name every idol takes flight and every demon and every unclean power: now let the demon that is here [in this temple] take flight at thy name.'" MacMullen goes on to say, "And while John was saying this, all of a sudden the altar of [Diana] split in many pieces . . . and half the temple fell down."[4]

This, of course, raises the question as to why John did direct strategic-level warfare in Ephesus while Paul did not. The answer to that is very simple. It had to do with God's timing. The time was right for God to direct John to do it, but it was not right for Paul. In fact if Paul had attempted to do it outside of God's timing, he might well have been the one who was defeated, not Diana.

Just to underscore the blessing that strategic-level spiritual warfare can bring, the city of Ephesus, beginning with John's ministry there, became the center of all of world Christianity for the next 200 years! Ephesus is a prototype of the kind of city transformation that many of us have been praying for.

Notes

1. Doris Wagner, *How to Cast Out Demons: A Guide to the Basics* (Ventura, CA: Renew Books, 2000).
2. Cindy Jacobs, *Protecting Your Family from the Occult* (Ventura, CA: Regal Books, 2001).
3. C. Peter Wagner, *Acts of the Holy Spirit* (Ventura, CA: Regal Books, 2001).
4. Ramsay MacMullen, *The Christianization of the Roman Empire A.D. 100-400* (New Haven, CT: Yale University Press, 1984), p. 26.

Since Scripture teaches that Jesus defeated the principalities and powers on the cross (see Col. 2:14-15), is there really anything left for us to do except to claim Jesus' victory?

This is a very important question.

At one point we were carrying out a strategic-level spiritual warfare initiative in a certain city when a Christian leader there told us that we shouldn't be doing it. He said that there is no question who rules the city—Jesus rules the city. He argued that Jesus had disarmed the powers of darkness. The satanic power over the city was defeated on the Cross. Our city may be full of problems, he said, but Jesus will ultimately be victorious.

This brother was sincerely attempting to defend a biblical nonnegotiable, namely, the fact that God is sovereign. We can agree on that. We can also agree that someday Jesus will return and establish His kingdom here on Earth and that Satan will be cast into a lake of fire for good. But meanwhile, Satan and his demonic forces should not be ignored.

Understanding God's Sovereignty in Daily Life

We need to understand how the sovereignty of God works out in daily life. Our sovereign God has so designed His world that much of what is truly His will, God nevertheless makes contingent on human attitudes, decisions and actions. There can be exceptions, but normally God does not choose to step in and overrule human decisions, even when they are stupid. For a starter, look at Adam and Eve. God, in all His sovereignty, allowed them to make a bad decision, and not only did they pay the penalty, but the whole human race has been suffering for it ever since.

Or take Jesus' death on the cross. The Bible is clear that Jesus shed His blood and thereby paid the penalty for all human sin. The will of our sovereign God is that none should perish (see 2 Pet. 3:9). Nevertheless, salvation is not automatic. Human decision is involved. That is why God has sent us out to share the gospel with unbelievers and to persuade unbelievers to receive Jesus Christ as Lord and

Savior. Human inaction does not nullify Christ's atonement, but it can end up making the atonement ineffective for certain individuals whom God loves.

Getting Back to Satan

Now back to Satan. On the cross Jesus "disarmed principalities and powers" (Col. 2:15), assuring Satan's ultimate defeat. But while Satan is *defeated*, he is not yet *destroyed*. Even after Jesus' death and resurrection, Paul refers to Satan as "the god of this age" (2 Cor. 4:4) and "the prince of the power of the air" (Eph. 2:2). John says that "the whole world lies under the sway of the wicked one" (1 John 5:19). Both Paul and John were aware that Jesus will ultimately be the ruler of our cities. But their language indicates that they also knew that the degree to which the will of God is materialized in our cities and in our daily lives in this present age depends a great deal on how we human beings, through the power that God has delegated to us by His Holy Spirit, successfully confront and neutralize the prince of the power of the air.

The Bible says, "Lest Satan should take advantage of us; for we are not ignorant of his devices" (2 Cor. 2:11). It is important to understand Satan's power and his devices. Obviously, according to this Scripture, to the degree that we decide to be passive about Satan or to ignore what he is doing in our cities and elsewhere, he will take advantage of us! We thereby can become victims instead of victors!

Jesus gave His disciples authority to bind demonic principalities whom He also referred to as strong men (see Matt. 12:29). But human inaction can permit principalities to retain their human trophies and to keep whole people groups in spiritual captivity.

Taking the Initiative

Just as God gave us a digestive system, expecting that we will take the initiative to eat in order to stay alive, He has also given us weapons of strategic-level spiritual warfare, expecting us to use them to defeat the enemy. We can decide to disobey and thereby nullify the gifts that God has given us. Or we can decide to obey and glorify the sovereign God through accepting and using what He has given us.

Yes, I believe that even though Jesus secured for us the ultimate victory, there is still much left for us to do in His power.

Do Christians have the authority to confront higher-ranking satanic principalities just as they have authority over ordinary demons in individuals?

This question relating to the authority of the believer is, in reality, the principal dividing line between those who have accepted strategic-level spiritual warfare as a legitimate Christian activity and those whom I described in the introduction as laggards and who in all probability will never accept this innovation.

Here is the way that Francis Frangipane puts it: "I believe the Scriptures are clear: Not only do Christians have the authority to war against these powers of darkness, but we have the responsibility to as well. If we do not pray against our spiritual enemies, they will, indeed, prey upon us!"[1]

Victors or Victims?

This brings up a point that I made in the answer to the last question. Do we want to be victors or do we want to be victims? Frangipane goes beyond the issue of authority to the issue of responsibility. He says that the initiative is ours. If we use prayer—which I see as the cannon through which all other weapons of spiritual warfare must be fired—we can be victors. But if we take the passive approach, we can put ourselves in a dangerous position where the devil can gain the upper hand over us. Few of us would like to be there!

Luke 10 is one of the key biblical chapters describing Jesus' instructions to His disciples about dealing with the demonic. It tells the story of Jesus sending out 70 disciples to spread the gospel of the Kingdom. He had previously sent out His 12 apostles, which makes this new event sound like it applies more to Christians in general than just to a leadership elite.

Unbelievable Authority

When the 70 returned, they were ecstatic! They said, "Lord, even the demons are subject to us in Your name" (Luke 10:17). The thing that was unbelievable to them was the amount of authority over demons that they had been given. I find it interesting that, despite the fact that Jesus had told them specifically to heal the sick (see Luke 10:9), we read no reports of healings there (even though it is safe to assume that there must have been many of them) but only of deliverance. Spiritual warfare was uppermost in their minds at the moment.

Jesus called the 70 together for a debriefing. It would seem reasonable to expect that, if Jesus were ever to teach His disciples that there was a limit to the authority over demonic spirits that He had given them, it would be now. But Luke records nothing of the kind. There were, however, two specific points that Jesus wished to make to His disciples while the memories of their ministry were still fresh.

Clear Priorities

One of the points had to do with *ministry priorities*. He wanted to be sure that they kept spiritual warfare in the proper perspective. It is all too much of a temptation to become proud or arrogant or, shall we say, intoxicated with spiritual power. Jesus said, "Do not rejoice in this, that the spirits are subject to you, but rather rejoice because your names are written in heaven" (Luke 10:20). Salvation is always a higher priority than being delivered from demons. The bottom line is heaven or hell.

From another perspective we are looking at a difference between time and eternity. Salvation is an *eternal* blessing. It lasts forever. Spiritual warfare is, at best, a *temporal* activity. It is only when spiritual warfare contributes to lost people being saved that it reaches its highest level of anointing. We should not see casting out demons or pushing back territorial spirits as *ends* in themselves, although many good things do inevitably happen as a result. We should see them as *means* toward the end of helping people become all that God intended them to be. This was what Jesus hoped that the 70 would understand.

No Limits to Authority

The other point that Jesus made to the 70 dealt with *spiritual authority*. He said, "Behold, I give you the authority to trample on serpents and scorpions, and over all the power of the enemy" (Luke 10:19). The operative phrase here is "*all* the power of the enemy*" (emphasis added). Satan exercises his power on the ground level, on the occult level and on the strategic level. It does not seem as if Jesus had any intention of limiting the authority that He had delegated to His disciples to the ground level only, as question 1 implies.

My position is that the same authority which Jesus imparted to the 70, He desires to impart to His disciples—like you and me—today as well. Through the name of Jesus and by virtue of the blood that He shed on the cross, we have been authorized to confront dark angels occupying any position in the hierarchy of Satan. That, however, does not imply that we should do spiritual warfare, particularly on the higher levels, apart from specific assignments from God. In every case, before moving out in warfare, we should be totally confident that we are following God's direction and that we are synchronized into God's specific timing.

Note
1. Francis Frangipane, "Our Authority in Christ," *Charisma* (July 1993), p. 40.

Our usual concept of prayer is talking with God. How then can we say that "we pray against evil spirits" as, for example, Francis Frangipane did in his book *The House of the Lord*?

Our best starting point for answering this excellent question is the dictionary definition of prayer. Webster says that "prayer" means "a devout petition to God or an object of worship"; or "a spiritual communion with God or an object of worship, as in supplication, thanksgiving, or adoration."[1] This makes it very clear that we do none of the above with evil spirits. Others do. Satanists pray to Satan. Hindus pray to a number of gods on their god shelf. Native American shamans pray to the "Great Spirit." Christians pray only to God.

That is why Francis Frangipane was very careful with his wording when he said that we pray *against* evil spirits.[2] It would have been a mistake if he said that we pray *to* evil spirits. We do not petition demons or ask them for favors. However, we do verbally confront them, and we cast them out if they are demons in individuals or we push them back and neutralize their power if they are territorial spirits.

Directing Warfare Prayer to God
There are two ways that we go about this. One is directing our warfare prayer to God Himself. Jesus prayed this to the Father when He said, "I do not pray that You should take [my disciples] out of the world, but that You should keep them from the evil one" (John 17:15). He also instructed us to pray in the Lord's Prayer: "Deliver us from the evil one" (Matt. 6:13). One way of understanding the apostle John's prayer in the temple of Diana of the Ephesians (see question 1) is in the sense of a petition to God. He said, "Oh, God . . . let the demon that is here take flight."

Issuing the "Prayer of Command"
The other way to pray against evil spirits is to issue a command to the evil spirit under the authority of the name of Jesus. Because this involves addressing a being in the invis-

ible world, it has been referred to from time to time as a prayer of command. This is not the way a dictionary would define "prayer," so it might not be the best choice of terminology. When it is used, however, we should understand it as an attack on the demonic spirit, not as a petition.

A good biblical example of this is Paul's ministry of deliverance in Philippi. While he was there, a spirit of divination, also known as Python, was harassing Paul through a slave girl. He put up with it for a while so that everyone would be aware that a power encounter was soon to come; and when the timing was right, Paul addressed the spirit directly, "I command you in the name of Jesus Christ to come out of her" (Acts 16:18). This command worked, and the spirit immediately left the girl.

Praying Against Evil Spirits

The way I see it, verbally exercising the authority that Jesus has given us against dark angels is what loosely could be called praying against evil spirits. I believe that such communication, called by whatever name, is authorized by God and that it actually gets through to spiritual beings in the invisible world. They hear it, they understand it, and they obey the command if it is done under the anointing of the Holy Spirit.

Having said this, I wouldn't want to go so far as to argue strongly for the use of the word "pray" in this context. My friend Tom White is one who would not recommend using the word "pray." He says, "We do not 'pray' at the devil. We resist him with the authority that comes out of the prayer closet."[3] "Resisting the devil" is also good terminology.

Getting to Know Carlos Annacondia

The Argentine revival of the 1980s and 1990s has become legendary. Of the many dedicated servants of God who led this revival, none made a greater evangelistic impact than Carlos Annacondia. His influence has not only been felt in his native land of Argentina but also in the United States, in Japan, in Europe and throughout Latin America. Annacondia has not been influenced by the rational Western mind-set that is behind a good many of the questions raised in this book. He is much more in touch with the realm of the supernatural than most of us in the United States tend to be. Some 3 million souls have been saved through his ministry so far.

I bring up Carlos Annacondia in the context of addressing evil spirits because he is uninhibited, not in "praying" to evil spirits, but in rebuking them in public and with a loud voice. In fact he has a book which carries the title of what some refer to as "Annacondia's war cry": *Listen to Me, Satan!*[4] The subtitle is *Exercising Authority over the Devil in Jesus' Name*. I consider it one of the most important revival books of recent times, and I highly recommend it. But shouts of command to principalities, powers and even Satan himself are part and parcel of Annacondia's evangelistic methodology.

Notes

1. *Webster's New Universal Unabridged Dictionary,* Barnes and Noble Books edition, s.v. "prayer."
2. Francis Frangipane, "Our Authority in Christ," *Charisma* (July 1993), p. 40.
3. Tom White, *Breaking Strongholds* (Ann Arbor, MI: Servant Publications, 1993), p. 40.
4. Carlos Annacondia, *Listen to Me, Satan!* (Lake Mary, FL: Creation House, 1998).

Isn't there a danger that command prayers, such as commanding a territorial spirit to leave a city, could lead us into unauthorized areas of ministry? Shouldn't we call upon almighty God to do this?

This question relates somewhat to the previous question. When the word "unauthorized" is used, the implication is that it is possible for those of us who believe in and practice strategic spiritual warfare to move into areas that God has reserved for Himself. It might be like the big mistake that King Uzziah made when he burned incense in the Temple.

The only ones that God had authorized to burn incense were the priests, and Uzziah was not one of them. The king's penalty for ministering in an unauthorized area was to suffer from leprosy for the rest of his life (see 2 Chron. 26:21). It can be a serious thing to go outside the boundaries that God has established.

"Be Quiet and Come Out!"

Few dispute whether God has authorized His servants to command demons to leave afflicted individuals. Jesus told His disciples to cast out demons, using an active verb. As a role model, He gave the example of how to do this when He spoke directly to a demon and said, "Be quiet, and come out of him!" (Mark 1:25). Theologian Wayne Grudem says that "the New Testament pattern seems to be that God ordinarily expects Christians themselves to speak directly to unclean spirits."[1]

The question then becomes whether we are authorized by God to confront and address unclean spirits in general or just some of the unclean spirits. As we move upward in what John Dawson calls the "limited hierarchy of evil spirits,"[2] the Scriptures do not give us clear directions one way or another. My conclusion is that we are authorized to do battle against the forces of darkness on all levels, depending on the circumstances.

Meet the Strategic Prayer Network

Over the past decade or so, the Strategic Prayer Network, which I lead, has logged numerous incidents—probably well into the thousands—of intentional, planned and well-executed strategic spiritual warfare. More often than not these prayer actions include, among many other things, what we would call command prayers directed to some of the higher-ranking territorial spirits. The participants in this ministry of prophetic intercession, particularly the leaders, are believers of experience, maturity, wisdom and discernment. They hear from God. They would know directly from Him if what they were doing fell into the category of an unauthorized initiative. They all know about Uzziah, and they are very sensitive about not making a similar mistake.

We do exclude asking God to take action on our behalf. Sometimes God will assign us to move directly to the front lines of the spiritual battle. When He does, we do our best to identify the demonic spirits that we are dealing with, and we should directly command those principalities to leave or to release their hold or to stop some ungodly activity. Often the Holy Spirit will give us detailed revelation of things we should know or of procedures we should be using.

Call on God
But at other times, we address God. We beseech almighty God to release His sovereign power. We suggest that He dispatch warring angels to accompany us in our duties. We ask Him to reveal areas of needed repentance or to guide us into prophetic acts. We, of course, do not *command* God to do anything. He is the master and we are the servants. But

He expects us to call upon Him for any action that He would deem appropriate for the occasion.

Notes

1. Wayne Grudem, "Miracles Today," in *The Kingdom, the Power and the Glory*, ed. Gary Greig and Kevin Springer (Ventura, CA: Regal Books, 1993), p. 77.
2. John Dawson, *Taking Our Cities for God* (Orlando, FL: Creation House, 1989), p. 137.

Jude 9 says that even Michael the archangel would not bring a reviling accusation against Satan. Isn't this a biblical indication that we should steer away from strategic-level spiritual warfare?

Many opponents of strategic-level spiritual warfare will quote Jude 9 and rest their case. It sounds so plausible that for many it becomes decisive. But the sound of this argument is much more convincing than its substance. For the sake of many who might otherwise be sidetracked by Jude 9, the answer to this question will be a bit longer than most.

Let's begin by refreshing our memory of the text itself.

Likewise also these dreamers [i.e., ungodly men (see v. 4)] defile the flesh, reject authority, and speak evil of dignitaries. Yet Michael the archangel, in contending with the devil, when he disputed about the body of Moses, dared not bring against him a reviling accusation, but said, "The Lord rebuke you!" (Jude 8-9).

There are several reasons why these verses should not be used to call strategic-level spiritual warfare into question.

What Authority Has God Given Us?

Jude's purpose in this short letter is not to address issues of what we know today as strategic-level spiritual warfare. It is not like another sixth chapter of Ephesians. Instead, he writes in order to warn believers against some false teachers who have appeared in certain segments of the Body of Christ. These people, whom Jude refers to as "ungodly men," have spirits of rebellion. They insist on resisting authority. They are definitely moving in areas which I spoke of in the last question as being outside of God's authorization.

I think it is important at this point to defer to respected biblical scholarship. Wayne Grudem of Trinity Evangelical Divinity School has given careful consideration to Jude 9. He concludes, "The lesson in this verse is simply, 'Don't try to go beyond the authority God has given you!' When Jude verse 9 is viewed in this way, the only question that arises for a Christian is, 'What authority has God given us over demonic forces?' And the rest of the New Testament speaks clearly to that in several places."[1]

Why Is It Important to Keep the Primary over the Secondary?

What this implies is that we must not derive significant conclusions, such as this one, from Scripture verses where a secondary point is made in order to support a primary point. This is especially so when the secondary point seems to be at odds with other Scriptures that deal with it as a primary point. This primary point has to do with the degree of authority that God has given us over demonic forces.

Both Peter and James, for example, instruct us explicitly to resist the devil himself. Peter says, "Your adversary the devil walks about like a roaring lion, seeking whom he may devour. Resist him" (1 Pet. 5:8-9). James says, "Resist the devil and he will flee from you" (Jas. 4:7). Neither Peter nor James hints that we should only ask God to resist the devil for us but, rather, that the burden for doing this rests with our personal initiative.

The pattern for this was established by Jesus. Wayne Grudem goes on to say, "During Jesus' earthly ministry, when He sent the 12 disciples ahead of Him to preach the kingdom of God, *He gave them power over all demons*" (Luke 9:1, emphasis added).[2] It would not be proper to regard Jude as attempting to nullify in any way what Peter, James and Jesus teach.

Should We Address Satan?

Let's look at Jude 9 more closely. There is nothing there about demons, whether demons assigned to individuals or demons assigned to territories. The only reference to a supernatural being is to the devil, or Satan. The crux of the matter, as far as Jude 9 is concerned, is not whether we should confront and address high-ranking principalities and powers who serve under Satan but whether we are authorized to address Satan himself.

Among members of the Strategic Prayer Network there are differences of opinion as to whether we should attempt to confront and address Satan himself. Some do use the name Satan, but mostly in a rhetorical sense. When they say, "I come against you, Satan, in the name of Jesus," they ordinarily don't imagine that Satan himself is listening to them because Satan is not omniscient and omnipresent. He is not God. Satan is a creature, and he can only be in one place at one time. What they do intend is to speak against Satan's empire of evil. It is like a soldier on the way to the Gulf War saying "We're coming to get you, Saddam!" In My answer to question 4, I mentioned Carlos Anna-condia of Argentina and what has become known as his war cry: "Listen to me, Satan!" Whether Annacondia is using this rhetorically or literally I am not prepared to say.

Questionable Reports?

I occasionally receive reports from those who believe that they have literally encountered Satan in person. I must admit that I am a bit skeptical about these reports. Cross-examination frequently leads to the conclusion that they may have, indeed, encountered very high-ranking spirits such as Beelzebub or the Queen of Heaven or Python or Wormwood, mistakenly confusing them with Satan himself.

I could not state categorically that no one has ever done battle against the devil one-on-one because I would have no way to prove it. But I will say that it would most likely be very rare. My point is that if we stretched Jude 9 to apply to us today, it could only apply to the case of addressing Satan and not to strategic-level spiritual warfare in general.

What Are the Two Sides of the Cross?

Jude 9 brings up another very important consideration to keep in mind, namely the difference between the back side of the Cross (the Old Testament) and this side of the Cross (the New Testament). Huge changes took place when Jesus shed His blood on the Cross. The world has not been the same since. One thing that happened, as I mentioned previously, is that the final doom of all principalities and powers, and Satan himself, was sealed once and for all.

Jesus made a very significant statement regarding this difference in chapter 11 of the Gospel of Matthew. He first said that the least in the kingdom of heaven (this side of the Cross) is greater than John the Baptist who represented all those who lived on the back side of the Cross (see Matt. 11:11). Then, in the very next verse, Jesus said, "The kingdom of heaven suffers violence, and the violent take it by force" (v. 12). I interpret this as a clear directive to aggressive spiritual warfare.

Now let's consider Jude's reference to "the body of Moses." This sets Jude 9 in the context of the back side of the Cross before Jesus came and changed things so radically. In the Old Testament, believers were not given the same authority over the powers of evil that Jesus has given to us on this side of the Cross. Nowhere in the Old Testament do we find incidents of demons being cast out like we see in the ministry of Jesus and the apostles. Although we do not know that much about what has or has not been delegated by God to angels, we cannot discount the possibility that even Michael the archangel might have more authority on this side of the Cross than he had in the incident that Jude cites on the back side of the Cross.

What's My Point?

I have taken a good bit of time to explore the ins and the outs of Jude 9. My conclusion is that the verse should not be used as if it were a blanket prohibition of strategic-level spiritual warfare.

Notes

1. Wayne Grudem, "Miracles Today," in *The Kingdom and the Power*, ed. Gary Greig and Kevin Springer (Ventura, CA: Regal Books, 1993), p. 75.
2. Ibid., pp. 75-76.

In Matthew 18:15-20, binding and loosing are used in the context of exercising church discipline. Why do you associate binding and loosing with spiritual warfare?

Matthew 18 is the chapter in which Jesus gives instructions on how to deal with a brother or sister who has offended you. You go to them personally; then, if necessary, you take some witnesses; then you bring it to the whole church. If none of this works, you expel the unrepentant sinner from the group. Jesus then adds, "Assuredly, I say to you, whatever you bind on earth will be bound in heaven, and whatever you loose on earth will be loosed in heaven" (Matt. 18:18).

Connecting Heaven and Earth

An important principle behind this is that there is an ongoing relationship between heaven and Earth, between the invisible world and the visible world. In the Lord's Prayer, we pray, "Your will be done on earth as it is in heaven." As we serve God, He gives the instructions from heaven and we carry them out on Earth. In this case, His instructions are to excommunicate a believer who refuses to repent of a sin against another person. God lets us know His will, but we are the ones expected to take the action.

Many do not see this clearly because most of our English versions give us a slightly misleading translation of the original Greek. At face value "whatever you bind on earth will be bound in heaven" might give us the idea that we are in charge of first deciding what should be bound and then heaven will agree with us. A much better and more literal translation of the Greek is found in the *New American Standard Bible* which says, "Whatever you bind on earth *shall have been bound* in heaven" (Matt. 18:18, emphasis added). This makes it clear that the initiative begins in heaven. God doesn't do our will; we do God's will.

This principle of binding and loosing actually first comes up in Matthew 16, two chapters before Jesus brings it up again in Matthew 18. If Matthew 18 were the only mention of it, it would be difficult to apply it to spiritual warfare. But in Matthew 16, Jesus brings it up directly in the context of spiritual warfare, not church discipline. Let's take a look.

Understanding That the Messiah Has Come

Some regard the event that took place in Matthew 16 as the most important occurrence in Jesus' life between His baptism and His death and resurrection. After having His disciples with him for a year and a half, Jesus asks them, "Who do men say that I, the Son of Man, am?" (Matt. 16:13). They mention John the Baptist and Elijah and others. Then He asks them, "Who do you say that I am?" (v. 15). Peter responds for the group and says, "You are the Christ, the Son of the living God" (v. 16). "Christ" in Greek means "Messiah" in Hebrew. This is the first time that the disciples were confident enough to say in so many words that Jesus was the Messiah for whom the Jews had been waiting so long.

Jesus' response was to say, "I will build My church" (v. 18). This is the first time that Jesus had mentioned the word "church." Why did He wait so long? Because Jesus couldn't tell His disciples why He came until they first knew who He was. He came to build His Church.

Breaking Down the Gates of Hades

Here is where spiritual warfare enters the picture. In the same breath in which he says "I will build My church," Jesus adds, "And the gates of Hades shall not prevail against it" (v. 18). There is no question that the gates of Hades will *attempt* to prevent Jesus from building His Church, but they will not succeed. If the Church is to grow, the gates of Hades need to be broken down. This indicates a confrontation with the forces of darkness, or what we call spiritual warfare.

What exactly are these keys to the kingdom? Jesus says, "Whatever you bind on earth will be bound in heaven and whatever you loose on earth will be loosed in heaven" (v. 19). This is where binding and loosing are directly related to spiritual warfare.

Binding the Strong Man

The disciples had already heard Jesus use the verb "to bind." A few chapters back, in Matthew 12, Jesus was talking about warfare, namely, the conflict between the kingdom of God and the kingdom of Satan. He then says to His disciples, "How can one enter a strong man's house and plunder his goods, unless he first binds the strong man? And then he will plunder his house" (Matt. 12:29).

Jesus was carefully instructing His disciples about their role in extending the kingdom of God through invading the kingdom of Satan. Only the most naïve would imagine that an aggressive assault on the kingdom of Satan would be met with anything but a desperate fight. That is why Satan and any of his principalities or powers attempting to stop the spread of the gospel must be bound. By whom? By the disciples of Jesus who are carrying the good news to the lost.

Loosing is the flip side of binding. Binding prevents the demonic forces from doing what they intend. Loosing reverses what they may have already accomplished. Jesus used both terms when He ministered to the woman who had suffered from a spirit of infirmity for 18 years: "So ought not this woman, being a daughter of Abraham, whom Satan has bound—think of it—for eighteen years, be loosed from this bond on the Sabbath?" (Luke 13:16, *NKJV*).

Binding and loosing, therefore, are extremely important weapons which must be found in the arsenal of all those who desire to win the lost for Jesus Christ.

Journeying from Debate to Decision

This serves as a reminder of something that must be repeated frequently. Strategic-level spiritual warfare is never to be seen as an end in itself; rather, it is a means to the end of world evangelization. When we realize that the eternal destiny of people may turn on whether we decide to obey Jesus and engage the enemy on all levels, we begin to realize that we'd better turn from debate to decision. This is what Jesus taught His disciples, and His disciples obeyed their Master.

As He did His disciples, Jesus commands us to cast demons out of people, but He gives no explicit command to cast demons out of cities or territories. Therefore, shouldn't we restrict our ministry of spiritual warfare to delivering individuals?

Jesus did command His disciples to cast out demons. One of the best-known Scriptures for this is Mark 16:17 where He says, "And these signs will follow those who believe: In

My name they will cast out demons." It is interesting that, at least in this case, when Jesus began listing signs of the Kingdom he listed casting out demons as number one.

In fact, the very first time that Jesus sent His disciples out on their own, He "gave them power over unclean spirits, to cast them out" (Matt. 10:1). Who were these "unclean spirits" that Jesus mentioned? What level of spiritual warfare was He talking about? Were they ground-level demons? Were they occult-level forces of darkness? Were they territorial spirits? The obvious answer to those questions is that Jesus didn't specify. All of them, however, would logically be included in the general overall category of "unclean spirits."

The Spirit Named Legion

Shortly before Jesus sent out His disciples, they had been with Him when He cast the spirit named Legion out of the demonized man who lived in the cemetery in the country of the Gadarenes. This story is told by Matthew (chapter 8), Mark (chapter 5) and Luke (chapter 8), and each account gives some details that we do not find in the others. The upshot of all the stories is that here we are not dealing with your average demon who may cause an individual to be in bondage to anger or lust or greed or infirmity or whatever but, rather, to something much more ominous.

The fact that Jesus interrogated this collection of evil spirits and found that their name was Legion was the first clue that this was one of the higher-level cases. Another was their request that "he would not send them out of the country" (Mark 5:10). Here we have a clear reference to a geographical territory, namely, "the country." So while the demons were clearly inhabiting a human being, they also had some important identification with a territory. Indeed, Jesus decided not to cast them out of the territory but rather into a herd of swine.

I mention this because dealing with Legion had to be fresh in the minds of the disciples when Jesus sent them out on their own with "power and authority over all demons" (Luke 9:1).

It is true that Jesus did not specify explicitly that the disciples were to confront spirits on the level of Legion or other territorial spirits. But this should not be the basis for an argument that Jesus would have *prohibited* it or that strategic-level spiritual warfare is not God's will. There are many things we do on the assurance that we are in the will of God that Jesus didn't address at all. He never recommended speaking in tongues, for example. He didn't command His disciples to plant churches. But He did tell us to take authority over evil spirits.

The Definitive Word "All"

Does that authority include higher-ranking spirits? I have previously referred to Luke 10:19 which, at least in my understanding of the verse, is specific enough to answer the question. Jesus said to His disciples, "I give you authority . . . over all the power of the enemy." That word "all" is definitive. I realize that sometimes the word "all" is used in Scripture in a figurative sense, but I do not think that this

How do you know that there is some kind of organized hierarchy among demons? What are the different ranks in such a hierarchy?

As we study the places in Scripture that give us information about the invisible world of darkness, it is clear that not all demons are equal. There are some demons who command other demons. How do we know?

The Nature of Satan

One of the ways that we arrive at the conclusion that there must be a hierarchy of demons is to consider the nature of

Satan. I brought this up in my answer to question 6, but now we need to look at it in more detail. While Satan is extremely powerful, as I have mentioned more than once, he nevertheless is not God. God is the creator and Satan is a creature. At one point in time, God created the creature we know as Satan. Because Satan is not God, he cannot have the attributes of God. He is not omnipotent, or all power-ful. He is not omniscient, or all knowing. And, more to the point, he is not omnipresent—in all places at all times.

Because he is not God and only a creature, Satan can only be in one place at one time. He may be able to get from one place to another very quickly, but still he has to leave where he is now in order to get to where he wants to be. When we think about this, it makes sense; but very often we don't stop to think, and therefore we imagine that Satan himself is all over. When we are doing spiritual war-fare and we say, "I rebuke you, Satan," the chances are good that he himself does not hear us saying that. It's not like praying "Our Father in heaven" and knowing that God Himself does hear us every time.

The Number of Demons

However, while Satan himself might not be around us, we know for sure that there are supernatural forces of evil in our vicinity. These are evil spirits whose activities are ulti-mately orchestrated by Satan, and there is a huge number of them. No one knows the exact number, but the Bible does give us a clue or two. Many Bible scholars believe that about a third of all the angels whom God has created have fallen and they are now demons. In Revelation 5:11 we read that the angels around the throne of the Lamb numbered 10,000 times 10,000, totaling 100 million. All of the angels might not have been there at the time, because in Revelation 9:16 we read about an angelic army of 200 million. If we take the 200 million figure to mean good angels, that means that there would be something like 100 million dark angels.

I'm not arguing for the final validity of this figure; my point is that there are a lot of demonic spirits in and around the world. There are so many that they cannot all report to Satan personally. Therefore, in order to maintain the communication system in the realm of darkness, more than likely there is a hierarchy through which lesser demons receive their orders and file their reports to greater demons who eventually can get their message to their commander-in-chief, Satan.

Archangels
Another related way of arriving at the conclusion that there is a hierarchy of evil is to draw on what we know about good angels. We know that some of the good angels have the position of archangel, which by definition means that they have authority over other angels, just like an archbishop has authority over other bishops. One of these archangels is Michael (see 1 Thess. 4:16) who appears again in Revelation 12. Here we read about a battle between Michael and his angels against the dragon, Satan, and his angels (see Rev. 12:7). The plain way to understand this is

to assume that each army was organized the way military forces are organized, namely operating with an internal hierarchy.

This is how we know that demons function in a hierarchy of darkness. In my mind it is a sound conclusion. However, when it comes to actually defining the different ranks, I don't think that we can be so sure.

The Rankings

It would be helpful if the Bible clearly stated the rankings and the relative positions assigned to angelic beings, but other than mentioning archangels, it does not.

The closest we might come to this is Ephesians 6:12: "For we do not wrestle against flesh and blood, but against principalities, against powers, against the rulers of the darkness of this age, against spiritual hosts of wickedness in the heavenly places." Are these titles of positions within a hierarchy of evil? Some think yes and some think no.

Tom White Versus Walter Wink

Tom White is one who thinks yes. In one of his books he has a section entitled "Hell's Corporate Headquarters," in which he argues that a reasonable interpretation of Ephesians 6:12 is to assume a ranking of Satan's hierarchy in descending order. He sees the "principalities" (*archai*) as "high-level satanic princes set over nations and regions of the earth." These would fit the definition of territorial spirits. He sees the "powers" (*exousias*) as cosmic beings who arbitrate human affairs. He sees the "rulers of the darkness of this age" (*kosmokratoras*) as "the many types of evil spirits that commonly afflict people."[1] In other words, these would be demons that we deal with in ground-level spiritual warfare.

Walter Wink is an example of one who thinks no. He recognizes that there are different kinds of dark powers, but he says, "The language of power in the New Testament is imprecise, liquid, interchangeable, and unsystematic. An author uses the same word differently in different contexts, or several different words for the same idea."[2] He points out how keywords used in the Greek New Testament for the powers, such as *archon, exousia, dynamis, kyriotes* and others, are not used as consistently as we might wish. Wink's conclusion, therefore, is that we should not try to arrange these in some hierarchical order

To be honest, I see some merit in each of the arguments I have cited. This is one of those areas where I would not want to be overly dogmatic. I suppose that I find myself leaning slightly toward Walter Wink and using a good bit of caution in attempting to name the different ranks in Satan's hierarchy. At the same time, I have no personal doubt at all that there is a satanic hierarchy out there which we must deal with when we engage the enemy in spiritual warfare.

Notes

1. Tom White, *The Believer's Guide to Spiritual Warfare* (Ann Arbor, MI: Servant Publications, 1990), p. 34.
2. Walter Wink, *Naming the Powers* (Philadelphia: Fortress, 1984), pp. 9-10.

Is it essential to learn the names of the principalities over a city as a part of the process of city transformation? How can such a thing be justified?

In looking at this question, we need to remind ourselves, first of all, that demons, evil spirits and principalities have names starting with their leader's name, Satan. Just like every individual whom you know has his or her own personality and his or her own name, demons are also individual personalities. However, they are not human beings; they are angelic beings. Each one is a creature created by God. They are not created in the image of God like human beings are, but they are created in the image God designed them to be.

Communication Among Demons

One of the implications of this is that demons communicate. We may not know exactly how they talk among themselves or what language they use, but in order to communicate they need to know each other's name. Numerous cases have been recorded and verified of demons speaking to humans in the human's own vernacular. In other instances demons have spoken out loud in a language foreign to the listener. Demons also respond to and obey human commands when the command is given with the authority of the name of Jesus.

A good example is Jesus speaking to the unclean spirit in the demonized Gadarene man. Using the man's voice the demon spoke to Jesus in vernacular Aramaic: "What have I to do with You, Jesus, Son of the Most High God? I implore You by God that You do not torment me" (Mark 5:7). Then Jesus spoke directly to the demon: "What is your name?" (v. 9). In other words, Jesus knew that demons have names. And, as we well know, this demon's name turned out to be Legion.

Old Testament and New Testament

Through many parts of the Old Testament, demons are named by name (see 2 Kings 17:29-31). The fact that these are often thought of as deities, or gods or goddesses with a small *g*, does not alter the fact that they are demons. They are mostly the higher-ranking demons that we deal with through strategic-level spiritual warfare as opposed to lower-ranking demons that we confront in ground-level spiritual warfare. But they all have names. Think, for example, of "Baal" (2 Kings 21:3) or "Ashtoreth" and "Milcom" (1 Kings 11:5) or many others in the Old Testament.

In the New Testament many demons other than Legion are also revealed by name. We have, for example, "Beelzebub" (Luke 11:15) and "Wormwood" (Rev. 8:11) and "Abaddon" or "Apollyon" (Rev. 9:11). It was very important that when Paul went to evangelize Ephesus, he knew that the name of the demon who had the city in bondage was "Diana" (Acts 19).

Proper Names and Functional Names

Names of demons can be either proper names, as are all of the above, or functional names. An example of a functional name comes up when Jesus heals a crippled woman on the Sabbath. He says that Satan had her bound for 18 years. Satan, of course, did not do this personally but, rather, he delegated the evil task to a subordinate demon which Jesus called by a functional name, a "spirit of infirmity" (Luke 13:11). He no doubt had a proper name as well, but it was not necessary that Jesus know or use the proper name when the functional name would do.

When Paul went to Philippi, he encountered an extremely powerful spirit. It had located itself in a slave girl and had given her the power to tell fortunes accurately. This demon talked out loud through the girl, and it had a name. Our English translators of the Bible decided to translate its Greek name, *pneuma pythona*, with a functional name, "spirit of divination" (Acts 16:16). However, as you can see even without knowing much Greek, a literal translation would be "Python spirit." Another way of wording this would be "a demon named Python."

As the story unfolds, the proper name becomes important because at that time Python was a well-known high-ranking spirit who guarded the oracle at Delphi. The oracle was a female priest located in the temple of Apollo. This was one of the principal centers of counterfeit prophecy in the ancient world. Paul, then, wasn't confronted by any ordinary low-ranking spirit of divination. He was confronted instead by a principality named Python. We know this because the proper name of the demon has been revealed. In this case the proper name is more useful than the functional name.

The Advantage of Knowing the Name

The question asks whether it is *essential* to know the names of the principalities over a city. No, it is not essential to know the proper name or the functional name in every case. However, there is an *advantage* in knowing the name if possible. It is better to know the name or names of the dominating spirits than not. Why? Let me answer by quoting from the *New International Dictionary of New Testament Theology*. Keep in mind that this enormous reference work is written by straightlaced biblical scholars whose driving interest is historical and linguistic analysis, not spiritual warfare. Here is the quote: "In the faith and thought of virtually every nation the name is inextricably bound up with the person, whether of a man, a god, or a demon. *Anyone who knows the name of a being can exert power over it*" (emphasis added).[1]

I have heard some people say that we cannot depend on statements like this because they are not in the Bible. I have never been able to figure out why some have a problem with extrabiblical knowledge. Most of what we all learn from kindergarten through high school is not found in the Bible, but that material has become a very important part of our lives. Human beings, both Christian and non-Christian, who have experience dealing with supernatural demonic powers know how important it is to know the names of the demons, and there is nothing particularly spiritual in rejecting this knowledge.

Discovery of the Names

How do we discover the names? This is a task of spiritual mapping. Sometimes the name of a spirit, such as Diana of the Ephesians, is obvious. Sometimes historical research will reveal the identity of the spirits. Sometimes God will give revelation concerning the spirits. Then again, certain occult practitioners who are serving the dark side may, for one reason or another, reveal some firsthand information about their masters. The Holy Spirit will provide discernment to know whether such information is valid or not.

I will not forget our pioneering effort at strategic-level spiritual warfare in Resistencia, Argentina, with Ed Silvoso in the early 1990s. Victor Lorenzo was the one assigned to do the preliminary spiritual mapping of the city. It wasn't long before he had identified the six demonic spirits who had been keeping Resistencia in spiritual darkness: Pombero, Curupí, Reina del Cielo, Freemasonry, witchcraft and San La Muerte. With this information, the intercessors led by people like Cindy Jacobs, Doris Wagner and Eduardo Lorenzo were able to target their prayers, bind the strongmen and open the heavens so that a significant degree of spiritual transformation could come to the city and its people. You can find more details of this case study in my book *Warfare Prayer*[2] and in Ed Silvoso's *That None Should Perish*.[3]

In his book *Taking Our Cities for God,* John Dawson reports a successful experience with spiritual warfare in Córdoba, Argentina. After considerable struggle, a breakthrough came when the team discovered the name of the ruling principality of the city. In this case, it was a functional name, "the pride of life." Once the intercessors knew that, they could come against it by ministering in the opposite spirit—humility—and they saw measurable spiritual breakthrough in Córdoba as a result.[4]

Notes

1. *New International Dictionary of New Testament Theology*, ed. Colin Brown (New York: Harper Collins, 1997).
2. C. Peter Wagner, *Warfare Prayer* (Ventura, CA: Regal Books, 1992), p. 32.
3. Ed Silvoso, *That None Should Perish* (Ventura, CA: Regal Books, 1994).
4. John Dawson, *Taking Our Cities for God* (Orlando, FL: Creation House, 1989), p. 19.

You mention the name of your book *Warfare Prayer.* Since that is not a biblical term, why do you use it?

There are several reasons why I think that "warfare prayer" is a useful term, even though we can't find it in any Bible concordance.

Spiritual Pacifists

In the Church today there are a considerable number of spiritual pacifists who would do just about anything to avoid conflict and warfare. For example, I remember a few years back when the United Methodist Church named an

official committee to revise their hymnal. On the committee were several spiritual pacifists who managed to persuade the committee to remove the classic hymn "Onward
Christian Soldiers" from the hymnal. However, when the
word got out to the believers in the pews that this was what
their hymnal committee was doing, they initiated a grass-
roots protest which eventually forced the committee to
change its mind and leave "Onward Christian Soldiers" in
the hymnal.

One of the reasons for this was that the Methodist
believers knew their Bibles. The Old Testament, for a
starter, is full of physical warfare, much of which was explicitly endorsed by God Himself. The New Testament from
beginning to end is a book describing how Jesus invaded the
kingdom of Satan with the kingdom of God. While Jesus is
known from the Old Testament as "Prince of Peace" (Isa.
9:6), in the New Testament He sees Himself more as a warrior. Jesus says, "Do not think that I came to bring peace on
earth. I did not come to bring peace but a sword" (Matt.
10:34). Jesus was no pacifist. He knew that true peace will
never come until the enemy—Satan—is defeated. Satan's
defeat began on the Cross, but it does not terminate until
he is cast into the lake of fire in Revelation 20. Then the
whole world will literally fulfill the desires of the Prince of
Peace. Until then, like it or not, we are at war.

Good Warfare
That is why Paul would write to Timothy and remind
him that he was called to be a warrior. He admonishes

Timothy that "according to the prophecies previously made concerning you, that by them you may wage the good warfare" (1 Tim. 1:18). He goes on to say that Timothy must endure hardship "as a good soldier of Jesus Christ" because those "engaged in warfare" must not be distracted (2 Tim. 2:3-4). Neither Paul nor Timothy was a pacifist.

In fact, when Paul wrote to the Ephesians, he saw their life for God as a life of warfare. The believers there were constantly battling the forces of evil under Diana and other high-ranking demons. When Paul tells the Ephesians to "take up the whole armor of God" (Eph. 6:13), he is using the analogy of the Roman legions. The Roman legions were well known for their aggressive warfare designed to expand the borders of the Roman Empire. Paul was encouraging the Ephesians to follow their example in the spiritual realm, aggressively extending the kingdom of God.

Since warfare clearly is not an *option* but rather an *obligation* in the Bible, I chose to use the word in my term "warfare prayer." I then attached the word "prayer" to it because warfare obviously requires weapons, and prayer is a major weapon of spiritual warfare.

The Spiritual Cannon

The Bible says that the weapons of our warfare are not carnal, but they are spiritual (see 2 Cor. 10:4). I agree with theologian and author Clinton Arnold, who concludes, "If Paul were to summarize the primary way of gaining access to the power of God for waging successful spiritual warfare, he would unwaveringly affirm that it is through prayer."[1] In fact—as previously mentioned—I would go so far as to say that prayer is a bit more than just another one of the weapons; it is rather the cannon through which all the other weapons of spiritual warfare must be fired. There is power in the name of Jesus, the blood of Jesus, binding and loosing, praise and worship, the Word of God and other weapons of spiritual warfare. But none of them will be everything that it is supposed to be unless it is accompanied by powerful prayer.

On the basis of these biblical concepts, I coined the phrase "warfare prayer," and I used it as the title for the first book of my six-volume Prayer Warrior Series.[2] Keep in mind that warfare prayer is only one kind of prayer. There are many other kinds. For example, Richard Foster has chapters on 21 different kinds of prayer in his excellent book *Prayer*.[3] Only two of his descriptions, authoritative prayer and radical prayer, would approach what I like to call warfare prayer. To quantify it, this means that a full 90 percent of the prayers that people pray are not warfare prayer. Foster's book and my book *Warfare Prayer* admittedly deal with a very specialized kind of prayer.[4]

One more thing. While it is true that "warfare prayer" is not a phrase found in the Bible, such a thing should not seem strange. For example, the term "Trinity" is widely used, but it is not found in the Bible. When it comes right down to it, the phrase "Holy Bible" is not found in the Bible either. Many other examples could be given to convince us that extrabiblical terms are acceptable so long as they point to biblical truths.

Notes

1. Clinton E. Arnold, *Powers of Darkness* (Downers Grove, IL: InterVarsity Press, 1992), p. 158.
2. The Prayer Warrior Series includes *Warfare Prayer, Prayer Shield, Breaking Strongholds in Your City, Churches That Pray, Confronting the Powers* and *Praying with Power*—all published by Regal Books.
3. Richard Foster, *Prayer* (San Francisco: Harper San Francisco, 1992).
4. C. Peter Wagner, *Warfare Prayer* (Ventura, CA: Regal Books, 1992), p. 32.

Terminology is one thing,
but there does not seem to be
any direct instruction in the
New Testament for engaging in
strategic-level spiritual warfare.
Doesn't this go beyond
the established bounds
of Scripture?

The way this question is worded seems to indicate that there may be an assumption out there on the part of some that whatever we do, presumably in the service of God, needs to be found someplace in the Bible. Let's think about that a bit.

Evangelical Christianity has never established as a principle that we must justify everything we do by pointing to an explicit biblical endorsement. On the other hand, it has clearly established that we must never allow ourselves to teach or do anything that is *contrary* to Scripture.

Reasons We Worship on Sunday

Take, for example, Sunday worship. Many Christians have chosen Sunday as their weekly day for worship, even though there is no direct instruction in the New Testament that they should. In fact, as my Seventh-Day Adventist friends like to remind me, Jesus and the 12 apostles worshiped on Saturday. Those of us who worship on Sunday continue to do so because we feel that we are not doing anything contrary to Scripture by choosing Sunday.

We take many other such things for granted. Many of us celebrate Christmas and Easter, for example. We build church buildings. We conduct Sunday School programs. We ordain clergy. We hold citywide evangelistic campaigns. We oppose the institution of slavery. Look over that list, and you will realize that none of those things is explicitly suggested by Scripture.

Knowledge of God and His Kingdom

Many of us continue to do these things with a clear conscience, however, because we feel that we know enough about God and about the kingdom of God and about bib-

xample, tend to develop their initial framework from the Gospels and move on from there. Many Charismatics, for their part, like to start with Acts as their basis for interpretation.

Through my early ministry I functioned as a dispensational epistle-oriented Evangelical. Consequently, I had blocked out much of the dynamic ministry of the Holy Spirit. I have now been trying to get away from that as much as possible. Once I began taking at face value the teachings of the Gospels and Acts, I could better understand spiritual warfare.

lical principles of Christian behavior to conclude t
approves of them. I say "many of us" because we all
be aware that every item on that list is or has been
to criticism on the part of some members of the B
Christ. They can argue that those of us who do the
disobeying God. Read their arguments and you wi
that they usually support their point of view by arg
that such behavior goes beyond the bounds of Scriptu.

One of my friends who was debating the issue
strategic-level spiritual warfare with me used this arg
ment. He said, "If Paul wanted us to do strategic-level sp
itual warfare, he would have said so in one of his epistles
He seemed surprised when I responded that if this were
principle, we would have to apply it not only to strategic-
level spiritual warfare but to evangelism as well. He was
surprised because he strongly believed in soul winning and
in evangelizing his friends and neighbors. But nowhere in
his epistles does Paul tell his readers that they should move
out and lead unbelievers to Christ. When my friend real
ized that this was the case, he quickly reconsidered hi
argument against strategic-level spiritual warfare.

The Gospels and Acts

I know that this seems strange to those who are thinkin
about it for the first time. How do we get into this min
set? Traditional Evangelicals seem to look primarily to t
epistles for biblical directions for ministry. They will oft
interpret the Gospels through the framework that tl
develop from the epistles. Other believers, Anabaptists

Paul may not have stressed evangelism in his epistles, but in the book of Acts we see him actually doing the ministry of evangelism. Why don't we see examples of Paul doing strategic-level spiritual warfare?

As a matter of fact, we do see several of those examples in the book of Acts. Questions like this come up from time to time because, at least previous to 1990, pastors and teachers were not doing much to instruct the Church about strategic-level spiritual warfare. Christian people in general knew very little about it. Consequently, when biblical scholars sat down to write commentaries on Acts, they were not mentally programmed to recognize strategic-level spiritual warfare when they saw it. It was not taught in seminaries and Bible schools, so most pastors were also ignorant of it.

Acts of the Holy Spirit

I taught the book of Acts for 13 years during the time that I was learning about strategic-level spiritual warfare. When it became evident that I had begun to see things in Acts that I couldn't find in the commentaries, I decided to write a new commentary that would address many of the pressing questions that were now being raised throughout the Body of Christ. I spent several years on this project, and a 550-page commentary, *Acts of the Holy Spirit*, is now available.[1] I will give you a sample of what I found, but I highly recommend that you secure *Acts of the Holy Spirit* if you are interested in understanding strategic-level spiritual warfare in greater depth.

The three most prominent examples of Paul engaging in strategic-level spiritual warfare are Acts 13 (Paul's ministry in western Cyprus); Acts 16 (Paul's confrontation in Philippi); and Acts 19 (Paul's evangelization of Ephesus and the province of Asia Minor). Let's look at them.

The Power Encounter with Elymas

Acts 13 is a notable chapter because it begins with Paul and Barnabas being sent out from Antioch to evangelize the

Gentiles. I find it interesting that the first actual story that Luke tells in the book of Acts about the incredible missionary career of the apostle Paul involves strategic-level spiritual warfare linked with evangelism. It might not be far-fetched to suppose that this could have been an intentional prophetic statement by Luke. In other words, Luke could have been setting forth, right from the beginning, a determinative pattern for Paul's subsequent ministry.

The dramatic power encounter that began Paul's evangelistic initiative in Paphos, western Cyprus, is recorded in Acts 13:6-12. There Paul had reached the highest political official in the land, Proconsul Sergius Paulus. When Paul began to share the gospel, he was strongly opposed by an occult practitioner, Elymas, whose assignment from the enemy was to keep Sergius Paulus and the whole region in spiritual darkness. Paul did not hesitate to confront Elymas and, through him, the spirits who were empowering him. Among other things, he sharply addressed the sorcerer as "you son of the devil" (v. 10). Paul proclaimed a temporary curse of blindness on the false prophet, and when the power of God came in such a visible way the proconsul was astonished. The result? Sergius Paulus was saved, and the region opened to the gospel.

Why is this regarded as strategic-level spiritual warfare? Ordinarily a power encounter with a sorcerer or a false prophet would be seen as occult-level spiritual warfare. However, this case is different because it was directly connected with a whole region and with the political authority over the region, the proconsul. It is safe to presume that the territorial spirit over western Cyprus, although invisible, would have been personally involved in the scenario. A defeat of the chief human instrument of the principality, Elymas, would have been a defeat of the principality as well. Evangelism, in this case, was very much tied in with strategic-level spiritual warfare.

The Spirit Named Python in Philippi

When Paul arrived in Philippi he found himself in a similar situation. This time, however, we know the name of the territorial spirit whom Paul encountered. As I have said, it is not essential to know the name of the spirit, but it helps. This incident is related in Acts 16:16-18. It involves a slave girl who was empowered by a "spirit of divination." Under question 10 I explained how our English translators chose to use the functional name "a spirit of divination," when a more literal translation of the Greek would have been "a spirit named Python," the proper name. Python was as well known by the people of Philippi back then as Kali is known today by the people of India. Python was associated with the temple of Apollo in the nearby city of Delphi, one of the most notorious seats of Satan at that time.

In the visible world, it might seem that Paul's confrontation was with a slave girl who told fortunes. But in the invisible world it was much more than that. Through the fortune-teller, Python had been fulfilling his assignment from Satan to keep the whole city of Philippi in spiritual darkness. What leads us to this conclusion? When Paul addressed the spirit directly and said, "I command you in the name of Jesus Christ to come out of her!" (v. 18), the impact of what had then transpired in the invisible world was not just felt by the slave girl, as it would have been if we were looking at a simple case of ground-level spiritual warfare, but by the whole territory. The issue was not just the salvation of a soul but the transformation of a city. The political authorities were so shaken by this that they had Paul and Silas beaten and thrown into prison.

Here again, strategic-level spiritual warfare was a vital ingredient of Paul's missionary work in Philippi. The result? Another strong church was planted.

Diana of the Ephesians

The most classical combination of ground-level, occult-level and strategic-level spiritual warfare is seen in the evangelization of the city of Ephesus and the province of Asia Minor. Here the apostle John finishes what Paul began. Paul's warfare is recorded in Acts 19:11-20, and John's experiences are found in subsequent history (see account in question 1).

I explained this in some detail in question 1, so I do not need to repeat myself here. I wanted to bring it up once again, however, because the question I am attempting to answer is based on the assumption that there is not much material on strategic-level spiritual warfare in the book of Acts, while there is a good bit of material on evangelism. My contention is that they go together. Look what happened here in Ephesus: "And this continued for two years, so that all who dwelt in Asia heard the word of the Lord

If we examine standard Christian theological works written across the centuries, we do not find sections in any of them dealing with strategic-level spiritual warfare. What do you think of this?

While God is sovereign, I do not like to think of Him as static. I believe that God likes to pour out new wine, and when He does, the new wine should go into new wineskins. I think that this is implied in the phrase: "He who has an ear, let him hear what the Spirit says to the churches," which appears no fewer than seven times in chapters 2 and 3 of the book of Revelation. This is present tense. God has spoken in the past and we constantly need to remind ourselves of that. But he also continues to reveal new things to His people. Theologians generally concern themselves with systematizing what God has said in the past.

The Lag Time Is 10 Years

As I have mentioned from time to time, the notion of strategic-level spiritual warfare did not begin to spread widely through the Body of Christ until around 1990. Even in these days of the information superhighway, it normally takes at least 10 years for professional theologians to place a new action or revelation of God toward the top of their agendas. Consequently, I would expect sections on strategic-level spiritual warfare to begin to appear in systematic theologies any day now (some pro; some con), but I am not really surprised that it is taking this long. To refer back to the diffusion of innovation theory that I explained in the introduction, theologians usually begin to pick up on issues toward the end of the middle adoption stage and throughout the late adoption stage.

By way of example, take the most complete and respected systematic theology to date of the charismatic renewal movement, *Renewal Theology* by J. Rodman Williams. This was produced between 1988 and 1992, a time when Christian leaders were just beginning to minister in strategic-level spiritual warfare and few people were talking about it. The book is 1,500 pages long, and there is no reference in the index to spiritual warfare or warfare.[1]

The mentality that we should postpone new forms of thinking or of ministry until the professional theologians first work them through is a recipe for preserving the status quo. Most of the significant changes in the life of the Church have come through pioneers who have experimented with them in real ministry situations. I agree with Ray Anderson, a respected theologian in his own right, who says, "One fundamental thesis will control this discussion—the thesis that ministry precedes and produces theology, not the reverse."[2]

The Ministry of All Believers Has Been Ordained by the Holy Spirit

Let me give you an example. Just about everybody I know agrees that the ministry of the Church should be done by the believers themselves through the spiritual gifts which God gives to every believer. The idea that only the ordained clergy should do ministry would be defended by very few, if any, these days. However, you do not find this in the standard theologies of the Church before 1970. It is not in the works of Martin Luther, John Calvin or John Wesley. Martin Luther popularized the doctrine of the *priesthood* of all believers, but he never understood the *ministry* of all believers: a big difference. The ministry of all believers is one of the most significant changes in Church life in all of history, but it did not come because our professional theologians suggested it. It came because there were many ordinary Church leaders who had ears to hear what the Spirit began saying to the churches several decades ago.

Theologians Are Spiritual Lifeguards

By saying this I am not discounting the role that God has given to theologians. I am just trying to put it into perspective. Theologians are like spiritual lifeguards who can keep us from crossing lines leading to dangerous heresies. But they generally work off of agendas previously created by pioneers, activists and innovators, usually avoiding such roles for themselves. That is why many theologians are only now beginning to address issues related to strategic-level spiritual warfare.

I can recommend one newer theological work which digs deeply into the theological implications of the ministry of strategic-level spiritual warfare developed in the 1990s: *God at War: The Bible and Spiritual Conflict* by Gregory A. Boyd.[3] My book *Confronting the Powers* is also quite theological,[4] but I am not regarded, as is Gregory Boyd, as a professional theologian.

Notes

1. J. Rodman Williams, *Renewal Theology* (Grand Rapids, MI: Zondervan Publishing House, 1996).
2. Ray Anderson, introduction to *Theological Foundations for Ministry* (Grand Rapids, MI: William B. Eerdmans Publishing Co., 1979), p. 7.
3. Gregory A. Boyd, *God at War: The Bible and Spiritual Conflict* (Downers Grove, IL: InterVarsity Press, 1997).
4. C. Peter Wagner, *Confronting the Powers* (Ventura, CA: Regal Books, 1997).

How about history? Do we have examples in Church history where Christian leaders used strategic-level spiritual warfare as part of their evangelistic advance?

This is a very important question, so my answer will be a bit long. It is a fact that standard courses in Church history taught in our seminaries and Bible schools have not included much material on strategic-level spiritual warfare. Not surprisingly, this has caused Church leaders in general to presume that we have few historical precedents. However, once we begin rereading Church history with a question like this in mind, many examples that reflect the principal thesis of this book do turn up, especially those connecting strategic-level spiritual warfare to evangelism and the spread of the gospel.

The Partial Nature of History

Before I give a few examples, let me introduce another thought. Suppose we thoroughly combed Church history and found nothing about spiritual warfare or territorial spirits? Even if that were the case, it would not be sufficient grounds to reject strategic-level spiritual warfare categorically. Why? First, because we cannot presume that everything that has ever happened was written down by historians, especially when the historians themselves might not have believed in strategic-level spiritual warfare.

Second, further research into historical documents could at any time turn up new material such as this. All historians agree that historical data is, by nature, partial. There is always room for new discoveries.

Third, it is incorrect to suppose that God does nothing new. God is sovereign, and He can begin this year or next year or any time in the future to do something new that He never did before. I gave an example of this in my answer to the last question in relationship to the widespread agreement that we now have on the ministry of all believers. We now live in the first generation when, as far as Church history records, the ministry of the Church is being delegated to and actually done by ordinary believers. Who cares if we can't find it in Church history?

Origin of Christian Rome

Fortunately, in this case, we have more historical examples of strategic-level spiritual warfare than we do of the ministry of all believers. One of our chief historical sources is Professor Ramsay MacMullen, a highly respected secular historian. He is the Dunham professor of history and classics at Yale University. MacMullen's specialty happens to be the history of the Roman Empire. A primary challenge of any historian of the Roman Empire is to attempt to explain how that empire, once having no Christians at all, within 400 years became totally Christian from the emperor on down.

Ramsay MacMullen rises to the challenge with his scholarly book *The Christianization of the Roman Empire A.D. 100-400*. MacMullen's remarkable conclusion is that the chief factor contributing to the spread of Christianity in the Roman Empire was *casting out demons*! The book is full of concrete historical examples, many of them, of course, involving ground-level spiritual warfare and occult-level spiritual warfare. But examples of strategic-level spiritual warfare are also cited. He speaks, for example, of "head-on confrontation with supernatural beings inferior to God."[1]

Going Head-On Against Demonic Principalities

MacMullen claims that we find a great deal of, to use my terminology, strategic-level spiritual warfare in history. He even gives reasons why some other historians may have refused to mention it in their books even though they knew about it. He says, "Driving all competition from the field head-on was crucial. The world, after all, held many dozens and hundreds of gods. Choice was open to everybody. It could thus be only a most exceptional force that would actually displace alternatives and compel allegiance; it could only be the most probative demonstrations that would work. We should therefore *assign as much weight to this, the chief instrument of conversion, as the best earliest reporters do*" (emphasis added).[2]

Let's take a look at a few of the prominent figures of Christian history who have gone on record as recognizing the importance of territorial spirits and of strategic-level spiritual warfare. I'll try to simplify things a bit and do it by century.

Second Century: Justin Martyr

In "Dialogue with Trypho," Justin Martyr affirms that there is a principality of darkness assigned to the city of Damascus. Not only that, but Justin believed that the same territorial spirit also had power over all of Arabia. Justin says, "That expression in Isaiah, 'He shall take the power of Damascus and spoils of Samaria' (Isaiah 8:4) foretold [that] the power of the evil demon that dwelt in Damascus should be overcome by Christ as soon as He was born, and this is proved to have happened."[3] The "power of Damascus" was obviously one of the "principalities" and "powers" that Paul wrote about in Ephesians 6:12.

The three wise men who came to worship the baby Jesus came out of that part of the world. Justin Martyr has an interesting comment on that incident. He says, "The

Magi who were held in bondage for the commission of all evil deeds through the power of that demon, by coming to worship Christ, show that they have revolted from that dominion which held them captive, and this [spirit of darkness] the Scripture has showed us to reside in Damascus."[4] Justin Martyr was one Church father who believed that high-ranking spirits do have territorial jurisdiction.

Third Century: Saint Gregory the Wonderworker

One of the most famous missionaries of the first centuries was Gregory, named the Wonderworker, because there were so many supernatural signs and wonders that accompanied his evangelistic efforts. His first convert, for example, was an occult practitioner who was accustomed to engaging in evil spiritual transactions with a demon who occupied a certain temple dedicated to Apollo. This demon was a principality known throughout the whole area as one who had, in the past, been invited to use the temple by a pagan priest. Such an invitation would afford the demon a "legal" right to the place.

Gregory actually was sleeping in the temple one night when the demon attacked him. The battle was engaged, Gregory had accumulated enough past experience in spiritual warfare to invoke the full power of God, and the demon was evicted. The demon later appeared to the pagan temple priest and told him that he had been sent out of the temple and that he could never return without Gregory's permission. When the shaman saw the irrefutable evidence that Jesus Christ, through Gregory, had the power over that well-known territorial spirit, "The priest's faith in the god was shattered. Returning to St. Gregory, he became a catechumen, and subsequently, by holiness of life, proved worthy to succeed [Gregory] as bishop."[5]

Ramsay MacMullen tells of another of the many experiences of Gregory confronting territorial spirits, this one with a fascinating twist. "And the [demon] himself, being enraged by the *territory conquered from him* by the bishop [Gregory], where once *both countryside and chief city were in the grip of demons,* inspires a woman to defame him. She is a prostitute, and accuses him as being one of her lovers, but he exorcises the evil spirit from her also" (emphasis added).[6]

Were there evangelistic results of Gregory's strategic-level spiritual warfare? He saw an abundant spiritual harvest. Historian Kenneth Scott Latourette reports: "When [Gregory] died . . . it is said that in contrast with the seventeen Christians whom he found on his accession to the episcopal see, only seventeen of the populace remained pagan."[7]

Fourth Century: Saint Martin of Tours

Martin of Tours, the famous pioneer missionary to France, spread the gospel by boldly invading demonic territory, such as sacred pagan shrines, and in front of great crowds by humiliating and shattering the power of the long-entrenched principalities of darkness.

In one village, for example, Martin discovered that the territorial spirit holding the village in bondage occupied a certain huge pine tree. Martin proceeded to challenge the demon by starting to chop down the pine tree. The people immediately rose up against him, and they challenged Martin to a power encounter. They dared Martin to stand to the side of the tree, where it was obviously leaning and certain to fall, and allow them to chop down the tree with him under it. If Martin's God was powerful enough, He would protect the missionary. Martin agreed.

The pagans, shouting and laughing, began to cut the tree down. The whole village had gathered to witness the spectacle. The huge tree suddenly made a loud cracking noise and began to crash. Martin calmly held up his hand and rebuked the demon-infested tree in the name of Jesus Christ. Martin's biographer, Sulpitius, reports: "Then, indeed, after the manner of a spinning top (one might have thought it driven back), [the tree] swept around to the opposite side, to such a degree that it almost crushed the rustics who had taken their places there in what was deemed a safe spot."[8]

And the evangelistic outcome of such warfare? "The well-known result was that on that day salvation came *to that region*. For there was hardly one of that immense multitude of heathens who did not express a desire for the imposition of hands, and, abandoning his impious errors, made a profession of faith in the Lord Jesus" (emphasis added).[9]

Sixth Century: Saint Benedict of Nursia

Benedict has gone down in history as the founder of monasticism. To this day, many orders of monks follow variations of his *Benedictine Rule*, which he wrote at his monastery on Monte Cassino in Italy.

When Benedict secured Monte Cassino, he found that it had long ago become a notorious center of witchcraft, idolatry and pagan rites. Deities such as Venus and Jupiter and Mithra and Apollo were regularly worshiped there. Many regarded it as a seat of Satan.

Monte Cassino was a spiritual challenge for Benedict, like waving a red flag in front of a bull. His first act when he arrived was to complete a 40-day fast. Then he began to evangelize, and he won some of those living there to the Lord. Ready for spiritual warfare, he chose to focus on Apollo, one of the highest-ranking spirits under Satan. Here is how Hugh Edmund Ford describes Benedict's battle plan: "The man of God, coming hither, beat in pieces the idol of Apollo, overthrew the altar, set fire on the woods, and in the temple of Apollo built the oratory of St. Martin. On this spot the saint built his monastery."[10]

Once again the evangelistic results were incredible. Not just a few souls were saved but a whole territory, dominated for centuries by the principalities of darkness, was set free. Saint Benedict's biographer, Theodore Maynard, says, "Every last vestige of paganism was eradicated from the plateau that towered over the district."[11]

Eighth Century: Saint Boniface Battles Thor and His Oak Tree

Boniface was an English missionary evangelizing the pagan region of Hesse in Germany. When he arrived, he found an animistic people group which for untold generations had worshiped a territorial spirit named Thor. Boniface, who had already been through several episodes of spiritual warfare by then, knew that if he was going to see a significant move of God for the salvation of the Hessian people, he had to engage in strategic-level spiritual warfare and do battle with Thor himself.

He discovered that the central physical power point for Thor, his evil activities and his command of other demonic forces was an ancient oak tree, around which the Hessians would habitually worship the powers of darkness. Boniface decided to take the direct approach. He issued a public head-on challenge to Thor at the site of the oak tree. Boniface's weapon of warfare was nothing but an axe, with which he commenced to chop down Thor's oak. A huge crowd had gathered to witness the power encounter, fully expecting the mighty power of Thor to destroy the missionary.

Quite the contrary! Even before Boniface had actually cut the tree through, a huge supernatural burst of wind sent the tree crashing to the ground, breaking it into four pieces! The people immediately recognized that the hand of the true God whom Boniface preached had humiliated Thor and broken his power over the territory. Kenneth Scott Latourette says, "The pagan bystanders, who had been cursing the desecrator, were convinced of the power of the new faith. . . . [This] episode may well have proved decisive evidence in terms which the populace could understand of the superior might of the God of the Christians."[12]

Shortly thereafter, the Hessians experienced what mis-siologists call a people movement. They all rejected Thor and instead directed their allegiance to Jesus Christ.

I must again apologize for such a long answer to the question. But I felt that it was important to reread some of history, and in doing so there can be little doubt that God has used strategic-level spiritual warfare in conjunction with effective evangelism through the ages.

Notes

1. Ramsay MacMullen, *Christianizing the Roman Empire A.D. 100-400* (New Haven, CT: Yale University Press, 1984), p. 87.
2. Ibid., p. 27.
3. Justin Martyr, "Dialogue with Trypho," in *The Ante-Nicene Fathers*, ed. Alexander Roberts and James Donaldson (Grand Rapids, MI: William B. Eerdmans Publishing Company, 1978), 1:238.
4. Ibid.
5. W. Telfer, "The Latin Life of St. Gregory Thaumaturgus," *The Journal of Theological Studies*, no. 31 (1929-1930), pp. 152-153.
6. MacMullen, *Christianizing the Roman Empire*, p. 60.
7. Kenneth Scott Latourette, *The First Five Centuries* (Grand Rapids, MI: Zondervan Publishing House, 1970), p. 89.
8. Sulpitius Severus, *Life of St. Martin, Classics of Christian Missions*, ed. Francis M. DuBose (Nashville, TN: Broadman Press, 1979), pp. 121-122.
9. Ibid.
10. Hugh Edmund Ford, "Benedict of Nursia," in *The Catholic Encyclopedia*, ed. Charles G. Herbermann, et al., vol. II (New York: Robert Appleton Company, 1907), p. 471.
11. Theodore Maynard, *Saint Benedict and His Monks* (London, England: Staples Press Limited, 1956), p. 37.
12. Kenneth Scott Latourette, *The First Five Centuries* (Grand Rapids, MI: Zondervan Publishing House, 1970), n.p.

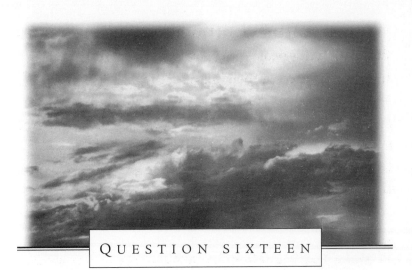

Preaching the gospel has always been the divine method of evangelism. Only the gospel saves. Why should we consider adding anything like spiritual warfare to it?

This is a very important question because it gives us a good opportunity to clarify that spiritual warfare is not evangelism. No one was ever saved by binding the strong man (see Matt. 12:29). People are only saved by responding positively to the presentation of the gospel of Jesus Christ. The message of salvation is that Jesus died on the cross for our sins. He is ready to forgive unbelievers of their sins if they believe that message, repent of their sins and accept Jesus Christ as their Savior and Lord. When they do, they are born again and they become new creatures in Christ Jesus.

As the question correctly implies, nothing can be added to this simple plan of salvation. So there must be no thought that spiritual warfare is a means of getting people saved or is in any way a substitute for preaching the gospel.

Identifying Obstacles to Evangelism

I think that we would agree that very few are satisfied with the current progress of evangelism in their cities and neighborhoods. In fact, it can become very frustrating to know that God loves the unbelievers around us, that He is not willing that any of them should perish and that still so very few seem to receive the gospel that we try to communicate to them. What are the obstacles?

There are undoubtedly many different obstacles. But the Bible is clear on one of them. The apostle Paul, like many of us, was frustrated that more people were not getting saved. At one point this caused him to say, "But even if our gospel is veiled, it is veiled to those who are perishing, whose minds *the god of this age has blinded*, who do not believe, lest the light of the gospel of the glory of Christ, who is the image of God, should shine on them" (2 Cor. 4:3-4, emphasis added). Who is "the god of this age"? It is Satan who has under his command an army of demons, principalities and powers of darkness.

Engaging the Powers of Darkness

Satan is bound and determined to keep unbelievers from hearing and responding to the gospel. And he has considerable supernatural power to accomplish his purpose. But greater is He that is in us than he that is in the world (see 1 John 4:4). Satan's supernatural power cannot match the power of the sovereign God. God has delegated His power, for the task of evangelism, to human beings like you and me who are filled and activated by the Holy Spirit. One of the ways that we use this power is to engage the powers of darkness in spiritual warfare in order to push back the veils that they have placed over the minds of unbelievers.

But even if we successfully tear down these satanic strongholds, that does not save the unbelievers who have been blinded. It does, however, put them in a new place. Previously they could not even hear the gospel no matter how it was presented to them. Now, with these blinders removed, they can hear and consider the true gospel of Christ. Then they must make their own personal decision as to whether or not they will put their faith in Jesus Christ as Lord of their lives. If they do, they will be saved.

We, therefore, should not think of adding spiritual warfare to preaching the gospel, per se. But we should definitely use spiritual warfare to the fullest extent in the *process* of taking the gospel to the lost.

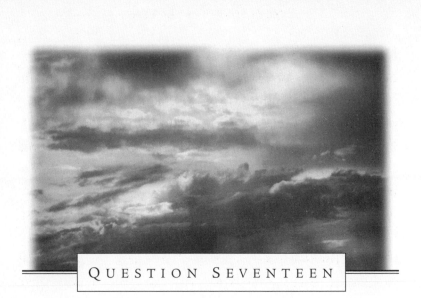

Directing so much attention
to things like spiritual mapping,
identifying territorial spirits
and prophetic acts can result
in giving too much credit
to Satan and the powers of
darkness. Why should we be
glorifying Satan?

Nothing that we do should glorify Satan in the least. Our chief end, as the Westminster Catechism so eloquently affirms, is to glorify God and enjoy Him forever. Unfortunately, some misguided individuals may seem to have a tendency to become so fascinated with spiritual warfare that it becomes an end in itself. In that case, it could well be that attention is directed toward Satan and not toward God. I would not want to be identified with such extremists, and I feel that it is too bad that a few of them can easily bring a bad name to the whole spiritual-warfare movement.

Spiritual-mapping methodology generally focuses first on discovering God's redemptive purposes for the city or other territory. Understanding what God's intentions for the city are directs attention to the glory of God and helps us target our prayers more accurately. The will of God and His divine plans have the highest priority in any kind of strategic-level spiritual warfare. Guidelines for doing this are found in John Dawson's excellent book *Healing America's Wounds*[1] and in Alistair Petrie's book *Releasing Heaven on Earth*.[2]

Affirming and praying toward God's redemptive purposes, however, must not bypass the need, at the same time, to discover the exact nature of the obstacles to evangelization and city transformation that Satan has erected. Paul says, "Lest Satan should take advantage of us; for we are not ignorant of his devices" (2 Cor. 2:11). Think of the meaning of this by turning it around. Suppose we *are* ignorant of Satan's devices? What will he do? He will obviously take advantage of us. No Christians that I know ever want to be in a place where they are vulnerable to the devil. One way to avoid that is to know clearly what Satan's devices are at a certain time and in a certain place.

Until the methodology of spiritual mapping came along, we had few tools to discover Satan's devices. Now we know how to go about it, much to the dismay of the enemy. He desires to keep his devices secret, or occult. But he is losing that battle. The best textbook on how to uncover the devices of Satan is *Informed Intercession* by George Otis, Jr.[3] And the best operator's manual, so to speak, showing us how to apply what we learn to warfare in our cities is Cindy Tosto's book *Taking Possession of the Land*.[4] We are more fortunate than past generations to have resources like these, and I believe that God is pleased when we use them to enter into the conflict with the devil. When we do, we are not glorifying Satan; we are glorifying God!

Notes

1. John Dawson, *Healing America's Wounds* (Ventura, CA: Regal Books, 1994).
2. Alistair Petrie, *Releasing Heaven on Earth* (Grand Rapids, MI: Chosen Books, 2000).
3. George Otis, Jr., *Informed Intercession* (Ventura, CA: Regal Books, 1999).
4. Cindy Tosto, *Taking Possession of the Land* (Colorado Springs, CO: Wagner Publications, 2001).

Is it possible for too much publicity about spiritual warfare to actually empower demonic spirits and make them more dangerous?

I have heard this question several times, but I have never been able to figure out exactly why some people seem to raise it. I would be equally puzzled if someone called into question whether or not we should continue doing research on the HIV virus and publicize the way it is transmitted for fear of causing more AIDS. Or why we should research the causes of breast cancer or of Alzheimer's disease.

The fact of the matter is that we spend enormous sums of money on medical research, not to *glorify* a certain disease, but to *eradicate* that disease. Experience has shown us that the more we know about a disease, the better we can fight it.

Exposing the "Wiles of the Devil"

In Ephesians 6:11 Paul says that it is important that we do whatever it takes to expose the "wiles of the devil." This is a method of weakening, not further empowering, the forces of darkness. "Wiles" is another word for strategies. Paul was wise enough not to be ignorant of the devil's strategies. Unfortunately, many believers today are grossly ignorant of them and therefore are more vulnerable to them than need be. Does the devil often get the upper hand? When he does, it is often because we have no idea of how he goes about attacking us, and therefore we get blind-sided.

Defeating the Enemy

Uncovering the strategies of the devil and publicizing them enough so that the whole Body of Christ is also aware of what Satan is doing is a strategic first step toward defeating the enemy. The more we know, the better, as long as we do not fall into the trap of either yielding to fear of the enemy or of worshipping the enemy. He is empowered by idolatry, when people pledge allegiance to him or ask him for special favors. But he is weakened when his ways and means of deceiving people are exposed. Secret societies, for example, are organized to give favor to the devil, and they cannot stand it when their secrets are made known. By the same token, broadcasting the results of our research into the invisible realm greatly weakens the forces of evil. It certainly does not glorify Satan—just the opposite.

Could strategic-level spiritual warfare simply be a fad? Couldn't it turn out to be like the discredited shepherding movement, which started well but later caused harm to the Body of Christ?

Yes, the dangers of abuse are there, and they must be avoided at all costs. It is questions like this that help us take the necessary time to build safeguards so that a movement involving strategic-level spiritual warfare does not succumb to the pitfalls of the past.

Let's see what we can learn from the shepherding, or discipling, movement. I was a missionary in Bolivia during its heyday, so I cannot speak firsthand about it. However, Paul Reid of Northern Ireland was a part of it, and he was among those who came out of it deeply wounded. He is also one of the few who has taken the pains to analyze his experience and record his findings in a book, *A New Easter Rising*.[1] In the book, Reid lists the three most troublesome aspects of the movement, all three of which he duly repented for practicing after he withdrew.

> Self-righteousness. We believed that we were better than other churches and fellowships.... Manipulation. Lives have been controlled through shepherding.... Idolatry. We have given to people the honor due to God alone.[2]

Self-Righteousness

Self-righteousness is definitely a temptation for those involved in strategic-level spiritual warfare, especially when it becomes clear that many conscientious believers choose not to be involved. In fact, some even choose to *oppose* it, and defensiveness becomes a temptation. When we feel strongly (as I do) that we have tuned in to something that the Spirit is saying to the churches today and when we come to understand that strategic-level spiritual warfare can lift the effectiveness of evangelism to a new level, we may easily become impatient toward those who do not agree. However, we must not yield to this temptation.

We may tend to forget that, in reality, only a relatively few members of the Body of Christ have actually been called and anointed to engage in frontline spiritual warfare. This calling is not rooted in some superior attainment of spirituality or some special status with the Lord. It is simply a matter of God's choice. A sovereign God has, for reasons known to Him, chosen us for a certain important task in his kingdom. Meanwhile, He has chosen others, and *not* us, for many other equally important tasks. In either case, the appropriate response is obedience to the Master. But our task doesn't make any of us better than the others.

It would be a grave error to project the elitist idea that only first-class Christians or first-class churches engage in spiritual warfare and that those who choose not to are thereby to be considered second-class. This is, indeed, self-righteousness, and God does not like it because it is a form of pride. The Bible says that "God resists the proud, but gives grace to the humble" (1 Pet. 5:5). Only if we remain humble will we be effective in spiritual warfare or, for that matter, in any other Christian ministry.

Manipulation

Fortunately, I have not seen this so far in the spiritual-warfare movement. That is not to say that control and manipulation cannot easily enter, because they can. But the Strategic Prayer

Network is under the kind of apostolic leadership that refuses to allow a legal hierarchy to evolve. Spiritual covering is regarded as a necessity in the lives and ministries of prophetic intercessors, but it is not the kind of authority-submission relationship that was seen in the shepherding movement. Coordination is vital, but control is not permitted.

Idolatry

While I might not agree that this particular sin should be called idolatry, nevertheless it is an important issue that must be faced. Just about every movement that I have been involved with through the years carries this inherent temptation. In the church-growth movement, certain pastors of large, growing megachurches received excessive glory. In the areas of power ministries, those who receive the most prophecies and those who see the most people slain in the Spirit are susceptible to this kind of adulation. In the spiritual-warfare movement, it is all too easy to exalt unduly those who may have seen the most spiritual transformation in their cities or those who have been chosen to appear on documentary videos.

If we are willing to learn from the mistakes of other movements like the discipling, or shepherding, movement—mistakes that their top leaders now freely confess—we can thereby avoid the possibility of becoming harmful to the Body of Christ. Our desire is to be harmful only to the kingdom of darkness!

Isn't there risk in confronting high-ranking principalities as Paul and Silas did in Philippi? They ended up beaten and thrown into jail. Shouldn't Christians just take a defensive posture and "stand," as it says in Ephesians 6:13? Is it possible that some of us could become needless casualties of war?

Now that we have several years of field experience with strategic-level spiritual warfare, it is possible to point to cases where casualties have occurred. This has caused some Christian leaders to become concerned enough for the safety of other believers to cause them to sound warnings against engaging in strategic-level warfare.

Keeping Casualties to a Minimum

Some have asked how we can do spiritual warfare without any casualties. I do not know. Warfare is warfare, and all warfare runs the risk of casualties. Having said this, I also want to affirm that those of us who are the leaders of the spiritual-warfare movement have the responsibility of keeping the casualties to a minimum. In all spiritual warfare we must avoid foolishness and carefully follow God-designed protocol.

For example, no one should engage in higher levels of spiritual warfare without the explicit blessing and covering of his or her immediate spiritual authority, in most cases the senior pastor of his or her local church. In some cases, especially on the higher levels and in locations at a distance from the local church, intercessors are well advised to seek out and obtain the covering of a recognized apostle. Pastors and apostles are in the government of the Church, and it is only God's government that can overthrow Satan's government.

Furthermore, it is inadvisable to attempt to do spiritual warfare alone. It should be done with a team so that many different spiritual gifts can be brought to bear on the situation at hand. These two procedural safeguards in themselves will go a long way to reducing the casualties of war.

Keep in mind, as I have said in answering other questions, that God has not called all believers to risk the dangers of the higher levels of spiritual warfare like He called Paul and Silas in Philippi. Those who thoughtlessly go into battle, especially on the higher levels, without being specifically called by God to do it, run the risk of become needless casualties.

Remembering Gideon and His Army

Think, for example, of Gideon's army. He began with 32,000 potential warriors to confront the powerful Midianites. By the time that God had sorted them out, 31,700 of them remained behind while only 300 were called into battle on the front lines with Gideon (see Judg. 7). It is notable that there was no recrimination on either side. The 300 did not complain that the 31,700 stayed home, nor did those who stayed behind criticize those who went. This is the way it should be in the Body of Christ today.

Personally speaking, I see myself as one whom God has called to the front lines. I do not regard this as any sort of a spiritual superiority on my part. It is simply an honest belief that God has given me an assignment and that my responsibility is to obey Him. But in embracing my own calling from God, I in no way consider myself better or holier than those whom God has called to stay home. Many of those who do are faithfully warring with Satan on different battlefields. Some, for example, have all they can do in trying to keep their precarious marriage together; some are struggling with dishonest business colleagues; some have been called to serve on an underfunded school board; some are stretching their budgets to care for elderly parents; some are working to plant this season's corn after an unusually wet spring; and on and on.

Giving priority to those kinds of challenges is biblical. God outlined His rules of warfare in some detail in Deuteronomy 20. Among the legitimate reasons why some who would otherwise have qualified to go to the front lines should have stayed home were those I have just mentioned. If they were building a new house or if they had planted a new vineyard or if they were just getting married, they were exempt from the military draft, so to speak. This shows that attending to such things as a priority is God's best for some, both yesterday in Old Testament times and today in our task of spreading the gospel.

Going on the Offensive

I tend to identify with the apostle Paul as being among those who are called to go on the offensive against Satan and his forces on the higher levels. Consequently, I attract others who have a similar God-imparted vision. I have given flesh to this in forming the Strategic Prayer Network in order to provide the apostolic leadership that a mission like this requires. In this role I need to resist the temptation to let my zeal and enthusiasm for the battle cause me to look askance at those who are not moving forward with

me. When I come across as doing that, I need to ask for-
giveness.

Caricaturing Spiritual Warfare

Some have argued that no Christian at all should move
into confrontation with demonic principalities and powers. Some have reprimanded us for exceeding the limits of
our spiritual authority. Some have caricatured strategic-
level spiritual warfare, referring to it as the big demon theory. Some have ridiculed "duking it out with the devil" or
"railing at devils on street corners."

This kind of language reflects, for the most part, an
ignorance of what actually occurs when spiritual warriors,
such as members of the Strategic Prayer Network, actually
engage the enemy. Those who use this language may not be
aware of the careful preliminary research, or spiritual mapping, that normally precedes such encounters. Responsible
spiritual warfare is done under the spiritual covering of
local pastors. It involves prolonged times of intimacy with
the Father, listening closely to God's instructions. There is
much praise and worship, times of profound repentance,
and sincere personal and social reconciliation. God is exalt-
ed and glorified!

Some spiritual pacifists attempt to support their position by characterizing the full armor of God in Ephesians 6
as defensive equipment, arguing that only one of the many
pieces is offensive, namely the sword of the Spirit. But it is
difficult to imagine that this is what Paul had in mind. His
analogy was the well-known Roman warrior of the day. The

Roman legions did not huddle in Rome waiting for the enemy to attack. They were deployed on the frontiers of the Roman Empire, constantly invading enemy territory and extending Rome's boundaries. Their armor was designed for offense. The defensive parts were only there to protect them from the enemy's weapons until they could get close enough with their swords to push the enemy back. Those called to strategic-level spiritual warfare today see their assignment as similar: pushing back the forces of darkness so that the kingdom of God constantly advances.

Realizing the Risks Are Real

Is it risky to do this? Yes, of course. Paul says to Timothy, "You therefore must endure hardship as a good soldier of Jesus Christ" (2 Tim. 2:3). As I have said, every war has casualties. Courage is required. Look at the apostle Paul who speaks of his own tribulations, needs, distresses, stripes, imprisonments and tumults (see 2 Cor. 6:4-5). But there is even more, namely, stonings, shipwrecks, perils of robbers, perils in the city, cold, nakedness, hunger and many other hardships (see 2 Cor. 11:23-27). Nowhere does Paul complain about being a "needless casualty of war."

Many of my friends who follow the leading of God into battle have suffered very much like the apostle Paul. By and large, when this happens they "count it all joy when [they] fall into various trials" (Jas. 1:2). They may get knocked down, but soon they are up again and in the thick of the battle. They know that spiritual warfare is won by the blood of the Lamb, by the word of their testimony and by *not loving their lives to the death* (see Rev. 12:11). They know their calling from God, and they enjoy living in obedience to Him, risky as it might be.

How would you respond to the suggestion that those engaged in spiritual warfare tend to substitute technique and methodology for holiness, evangelism and Spirit-guided teaching?

If this suggestion were true, I agree that we should not be doing strategic-level spiritual warfare. Our purpose for advocating spiritual warfare is to serve God by extending His kingdom. In all things we seek to honor God. Methodologies and techniques are means toward an end, and we cannot allow them to become ends in themselves. If someone thinks that they have a formula which underlies spiritual warfare, they are on the wrong track. Nothing that we do in the flesh will bear fruit. All must be carried out in the fullness of the Holy Spirit.

In answering previous questions I have made it clear that strategic-level spiritual warfare is done for the express purpose of removing demonic obstacles to effective evangelism. Jesus' Great Commission commands us to make disciples of all nations (see Matt. 28:19). He has told us to preach the gospel to every creature on Earth (see Mark 16:15). When we do this and when lost people respond to the gospel and become followers of Jesus Christ, God is pleased. He does not desire that one lost soul should perish but that all should come to repentance (see 2 Pet. 3:9). If confronting the principalities and powers of darkness expedites evangelism in our cities and our nations and our world, let's do it. Otherwise, it is not something that we should pursue.

Clothed in Holiness

Only foolish or inexperienced people would move into spiritual warfare without personal holiness. I remember Cindy Jacobs once saying that we can put on the armor of God, but that if we go into warfare without a pure heart under the armor, we will have holes in our armor. The fiery darts of the evil one will certainly penetrate and neutralize our efforts. I am so convinced of the need for holiness to be understood and applied in our lives that I have written a whole book on the subject, *Radical Holiness for Radical*

Living.[1] In it I attempt to make a case for embracing the Wesleyan view of holiness which affirms that it is, indeed, possible to live a daily life free from sin. I came to this conclusion only after beginning to move in areas of spiritual warfare and clearly seeing that opposing views of partial or incomplete holiness are no longer adequate.

Filled and Guided by the Holy Spirit

The question suggests that some overly zealous advocates of spiritual warfare might attempt to bypass the guidance of the Holy Spirit in their ministry. If this is the case, they do so at their own peril. The most experienced front-line spiritual warriors would not think of going into battle without the assurance that they are filled with the Holy Spirit. They know that the enemy is too powerful for them to move in the power of the flesh. They spend long hours seeking God and listening to the voice of the Holy Spirit, depending on Him for guidance every step of the way. They study Scripture and ask the Holy Spirit to show them how to apply it in their ministry.

After all, Jesus made the presence and the work of the Holy Spirit central in carrying out the Great Commission. He said, "You shall receive power when the Holy Spirit has come upon you; and you shall be witnesses to Me in Jerusalem, and in all Judea and Samaria, and to the end of the earth" (Acts 1:8).

Prepared to Fulfill the Great Commission

This was a good question to conclude *What the Bible Says*

About Spiritual Warfare. It helped us once again to affirm that fulfilling the Great Commission is central to our desire to employ strategic-level spiritual warfare as wisely as possible. Jesus came to seek and to save that which was lost, and our service to Him keeps this purpose central. When we have the gifts and the fruit and the power of the Holy Spirit in our lives, we are prepared to wrestle, not against flesh and blood, but against principalities and powers. We have the sword of the Spirit which is the Word of God.

My prayer is that all who read this book will be activated with this divine power that God wishes us to have. When they are, we can move out together to win multitudes of lost people to Jesus Christ, thereby spreading the wonderful message of the kingdom of God to our communities and to our world.

Note

1. C. Peter Wagner, *Radical Holiness for Radical Living* (Colorado Springs, CO: Wagner Publications, 1998).

Spiritual Armor for the Ultimate Victory

Deliver Us from Evil
Putting a Stop to the Occult
Influences Invading Your
Home and Community
Cindy Jacobs
Paperback
ISBN 08307.28007

Satan's Secrets Exposed
Overcoming the 14 Most
Common Tactics of the Enemy
Kingsley Fletcher
Paperback
ISBN 08307.28899

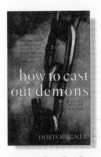

How to Cast Out Demons
A Guide to the Basics
Doris Wagner
Paperback
ISBN 08307.25350

Warfare Prayer
How to Seek God's Power
and Protection in the Battle
to Build His Kingdom
C. Peter Wagner
Paperback
ISBN 08307.15134

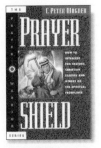

Prayer Shield
How to Intercede for Pastors,
Christian Leaders and Others
on the Spiritual Frontlines
C. Peter Wagner
Paperback
ISBN 08307.15142

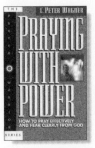

Praying with Power
How to Pray Effectively
and Hear Clearly from God
C. Peter Wagner
Paperback
ISBN 08307.19199

Also from C. Peter Wagner

Humility
Biblical Teaching on a
Misunderstood Requirement
of the Christian's Walk
C. Peter Wagner
Hardcover
ISBN 08307.29356

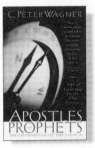

Apostles and Prophets
The Foundation of the Church
C. Peter Wagner
Hardcover
ISBN 08307.25741

Acts of the Holy Spirit
A Complete Commentary
on the Book of Acts
C. Peter Wagner
Paperback
ISBN 08307.20413

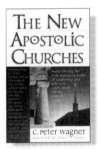

**The New Apostolic
Churches**
God's Desire for the
Church Today
C. Peter Wagner
Paperback
ISBN 08307.21371

**Your Spiritual Gifts Can
Help Your Church Grow**
How to Find Your Gifts & Use
Them to Bless Others
C. Peter Wagner
Paperback
ISBN 08307.16815

Finding Your Spiritual Gifts
The Wagner-Modified Houts
Spiritual Gifts Inventory
C. Peter Wagner
Questionnaire
ISBN 08307.17889